Anita's Piano

A story based on the life of
Anita Ron Schorr

By
Marion A. Stahl

*"No man is good enough to govern another man without that
other's consent."*
Abraham Lincoln, 16th President of the United States.
February 12, 1809 - April 15, 1865.

Luthas ....
CARY MY STORY
into THE FUTURE !!
LOVE

Legal Disclaimers

Book cover photo: Franze Grubner

The publisher has undertaken this publication in an effort to educate the public and younger generations so as not to repeat the past.
Any profit to the publisher will be donated to similar efforts.

Manufactured in the United States of America
First Published in 2014
9 7 8 0 6 9 2 2 8 8 9 5 5
4th Edition
Library of Congress Card Number
pending

ISBN: 0692288953
ISBN-13: 978-0692288955
E-Book: available

By the same author

A Modern Salem Witch Trial

The Monster Chase

Anita

Anita's Piano

Hope and Perseverance

(To be published by 2015)

The teacher's and adult version of the book "Anita" also contains reader questions and educator information relating to "Echo and Reflections", an excellent and acclaimed program sponsored by the Anti-Defamation League.

Dedication

This book is dedicated to the memory of Anita's family: her brother, Michal;, her mother, Stela; and her father, Fritz; her grandparents; and her dear Aunt Hilda.

This book was not written to stir up painful memories or to accuse but rather to educate future generations.

"Step up and be a Hero"

Anita's Family

Acknowledgements

I want to thank all who have encouraged me in taking on this subject, especially my husband for his invaluable patience and support.

This book would not exist without Paige Duke, Pat Folmsbe and Pete Eldridge's careful editing and her daughter Elizabeth Morton's computer abilities as well as Christine Rice.

I also particularly wish to thank :

Remy Benoit, retired history teacher and writer, for sharing her knowledge of the subject as well as the resources she used with her students. Her encouragement was a precious part of this endeavor.

Finally, we would like also to thank Judith Orseck Katz and Robert Herman, as well as the Anti-Defamation League, for their support of Anita's efforts.

Foreword

The world is well acquainted with the facts. However, the truth of the survivors, the people who lived through the Holocaust, has been neglected.

Anita and I met during a ski trip, and her enthusiasm for her mission to share her experience with young students moved me.

It has taken more than seventy years for Anita to share the feelings she experienced as a young girl. Her heart trapped every word of her experience.

Anita says: "I kept those memories locked up, feeling ashamed of them, for much too long until Elie Wiesel, Nobel Peace Prize winner inspired me. It was when I began speaking to schools. I would stop there if it weren't for the bewilderment and fascination I see in the eyes of the young students when I communicate my story. When I see the expressions on their faces, I know I have to do more to keep my voice alive. At the same time, I want to honor those who did not survive and ensure that history does not repeat itself."

Subsequently, her story inspired me and I decided to venture on a trip into history.

In school, I learned of the main infamous events of the time. However, the enormous losses were hidden from view. I lacked the knowledge of the devastation they had caused. I learned about the abuse of Hitler. I knew about Israel and Kibbutz, but the actual reason for their existence eluded me entirely.

Anita's story brought me much closer to understand how these historical events affected individuals and families, and their wounds bound in shame forever. We celebrated the fallen heroes but forgot the survivors: Heroes in their own right. Anita's message contains a lesson we need to learn.
Her story is not about accusation or reprisal. It is an effort to show how a lack of action to stop bullying may lead to situations spreading like a contagious disease. Bullying is a growing problem in schools and the cause of many teen suicides. Genocides still occur around the world. Anti-Semitism has made resurgence in Europe. Many believe that terrorism is a form of fascism as experienced prior and during World War II.

I sincerely hope that it will awaken in the reader a sensitive hero who exists in all of us. This book is about the devastating effects of the Pyramid of Hate.

CHAPTER 1

Song to the moon

Oh Moon on the deep deep sky
Your light can see far
You roam all the vast world
Looking in the homes of people
Oh Moon, stay for a while

Tell me, tell me where my loved is
Tell him, oh silver Moon
That my arm embraces him
So he at least for a little while
Remembers me in his dreams

Give him light on his way
Tell him, oh tell him who is waiting for him here!
Is the human soul dreaming of me...
Let him awake by the memory!

Oh Moon, keep shining, keep shining!

Music: "Rusalka" by Anton Dvorak

*L*unch is in full swing. The teenage girls, sitting at a long table, are busy talking. Their voices and their laughter are like bells, like notes on a grand piano. Light and melodious, they float the thick air surrounding us, as does the repressive unknown in our present existence.

We have been living on Belgicka Ulice (street), in Praha, Czechoslovakia, since May. It is near the Museum of Decorative Art, a large church, and the Univerzita Karlova.

I know my friends are trying to forget, but deep down inside our hearts, there is an unfathomable and immeasurable deep hole in all of us. Personally, I cannot ignore this void. I am submersed in thoughts, troubled by memories and the hope of answers that have been too long to come. I yearn for my mother's arm, my brother's soft cheeks, our laughter and closeness.

Daily, we go to a center where thousands of names are listed with hope to repeal our fate. Anxiously, we read through the long lists.
We are so hopeful and yet so afraid of what we may find. Our faces give nothing away, but we are shaking inside.

The light laughter and stories are just there to cover the horrible feelings we carry within.
"Anita?"

I am awakened from my deep thoughts.

"Anita?"

Mrs. Liron is standing at the door, dressed in her neatly cut gray suit.

Beside me, Ruth is telling a story to Ilse and Eva about what happened yesterday. She went to a job interview, and is recounting the experience in lively detail from the clothes she wore to the particulars of each event that followed. How a gentleman with thick glasses scrutinized her, interrogated by another, and eventually sent out without a job.
"Anita Pollakova?" The lady repeats.

I gulp another spoonful of the soup, and then another. There is no way I am going to sacrifice a drop of food to speak to anyone. Finally, I rise slowly from my chair. My cap, resting on the bench, falls to the ground. I had a haircut a few months ago, and I like wearing a cap to keep warm. It is now December, and winter is definitively with us. First, I pick up my hat, and then walk, unhurried, toward the large wood door that separates us from the rest of the world. The woman is still standing. Her eyes look hard. She seems to look right through the hole inside of me.

"Yes, I am here," I reply.

She motions for me to follow her. We walk through tiled hallways and enter her office. The room is neat. A picture of her children sits on the desk. They all wear big smiles and neat clothes, just like the picture my parents had done of my brother and me when we were little.

I take the seat she offers and stare at the floor. She is visibly uncomfortable. She is pulling her skirt, next her chair, then her hair. She starts to speak, but her voice isn't clear, so she coughs until it finally comes back.

The window behind her has a thin voile drape. I can see through it. The weather is smiling. The sun is out. A breeze is whisking through the branches of a tree.

I have lived here for over eight months now. It's just temporary, until my family is reunited. Some of the girls have been here for several years. Among all some were lucky, but others received bad news. I am still waiting. Since the news of my dad eight months ago, it has been a complete silence. The weeks and months have been so long that I have lost hope. I am ready for the worst. Yet, there is a glimpse of hope coming through these veiled windows, lighting the piano in my memories, as if it could bring back all the happy moments in my childhood, the memories that make my heart ache with longing.

"Anita," she starts. Her face is round and her nose is pointed. Her eyes are light blue with dark eyelashes. Her lips, bright with lipstick, are pursed in a grave look that concerns me.

"So far, we have not found anyone from your family: your aunt Hilda, your mom, your uncle. Nevertheless, we should not give up. Things are still being processed..."

I interrupt her, "What about my brother? He may not remember his name!"

"Well, I am sure. They would know how to identify him...and..."

I cannot hear the end of the sentence. Tears are trying to climb out of my eyes, but I am in stupor. I miss them so much. The pain is excruciating. The woman dismisses me without further notice. I feel annoyed, but of course, I must be one of so many. How could she feel for each one of us? I try to reason it out while I walk back through the gray hallways and many doors.

Since I learned of my father's disappearance, I turn at every silhouette resembling him. I am always ready to run for the slightest chance that it could be him. Every little boy has my brother's eyes. Every skirt resembles my mother's. I yearn for their presence.

I return to the table I left half an hour ago. They are still discussing yesterday's proceedings. Now, Ilse is giving the particulars of a difficult encounter with a sales lady:

"She says 'Return from where you come from young lady. We have no use for you...'"

My friends are a great comfort. Ruth and Ilse are my best friends. Ruth and I have been together for such a long time. It feels as if we are sisters. I am only fifteen, and she is nineteen. It is going to end. Ruth's family is on their way to take her. I am very apprehensive of their arrival as it means another separation for me. Ilse is in a very different situation. She is an orphan. Her father—and later her mother—were taken from her.

Most of the time, I carry my shield of armor, but I have difficulty concentrating on any one particular subject. I understand the necessity to learn. I even persuaded the principal of a private institute to take me in his school. I have achieved what he has required, but the longing for my family is so strong it is difficult to hear all that is being said in class, or to retain what I learn.

In our bedroom, there are six beds. Every night we speak late until we fall asleep. We talk about how we are going to visit together later, as if the world and time could not separate us. We gossip about boys and girly subjects, our growing bosoms and the color of our hair. We giggle under the covers to forget the reality of our circumstances.

I am fond of this boy who is in my class. Ruth is infatuated with her teacher. Eva does not talk much about what is in her heart, but she listens. None of us can imagine we are capable of arousing their interest. The humiliation and degradation inflicted on us has left it's deep, indelible claw marks in our minds and souls.

In spite of our insecurities and the austere living conditions we all share, we see ourselves living in castles and driving horse-drawn carriages in the years to come.

There is no limit to our imaginations. It helps sustain our disheartening present situation, the feelings of devastation and uncertainty ahead of us.

I have tried to contact distant relatives, but so far no response.

The "UNRRA" has given us clothes. I am into fashion now and decide to match my clothes. I dye my white stockings and beret purple to match the dress they gave me. We also received some shoes from the Bata factory.

Now that we have good shoes, we do more frequent trips to consult the sought-after lists. Hundreds are there looking at the same bulletin board. They look upset and sickly. Their old hats and worn clothes reveal their state of affairs. The sadness on their faces is immeasurable. After every visit, we return with a defeated look on our faces. Yet life continues.

In a few weeks, the lady in the gray suit comes again. This time she is very pessimistic.

"Anita, we looked everywhere. All the lists are in, and there are no traces of them. You are an orphan, and there is no other family."

I still refuse to believe her and know this is impossible. I leave her office more determined than ever to find them myself. A few days later, Ruth's parents come, and she leaves us. Then, Ilse is taken to a new family's home. They will take care of her from this day forward. Our good-byes are effusive, and the emptiness that follows is like a day without food. I am starving for "love." There is Eva, but she is quiet.

I feel like a broken cup glued time and again. However, the bottom is still missing some important pieces. I feel my family right next to me. I hear their voices, my father's singing. Life will never be the same without them. My longing for my family is beyond words. Nevertheless, I continue to consult the lists daily, hoping for a mistake.

I keep looking at everyone on the streets hoping for a miracle. How can I continue with all these missing pieces? My soul feels shattered.

CHAPTER 2

Anita

Anita: 1933

*I*n the town of Brno, (Br-no) on Monday, August 11, 1930, a warm summer day there is a celebration. Fritz (Bedřich) and Stela Pollak are welcoming their first daughter. They name her Anita. Her eyes look at everyone with a piercing insistence, not the vague gazes of most babies. Her gurgle of happiness makes everyone smile.

At this time, Czechoslovakia is the largest Eastern European country outside Russia.

President Herbert Hoover goes before the United States Congress to ask for a $150 million public works program to help create jobs and to stimulate the American economy.

Nurse Ellen Church has recently become the world's first flight attendant, working on a Boeing Air Transport trimotor.

It is what my family tells me about that day and that year. My Aunt Hilda, who has flamboyant, crimson hair and white skin, conveys how my parents, Fritz and Stela, had met at the Sport Hall on Kounicová Street in 1924. I am seven years old and wearing a green and pink outfit Hilda made me. It is a spring day. The park of the castle is redolent with flowers and filled with birds telling their stories. Sitting next to me on a bench in the park, my aunt is telling me the story of that important day.

"Anita," says Hilda, "On that Saturday, at the Sports Hall, Stela, your mother, was wearing that cherry dress with fine finishing. I also made a small hat with a band, in a paler tone of the same color. Stela worked with me. She helped me with sewing and various aspects of the millinery shop."

Aunt Hilda holds my hand and continues the story as if she is reading a book, and the whole scene is unfolding in front of her eyes.

"Stela was walking, accompanied by her friend Elisa. Two young men, about the same age, approached them. They were nicely dressed and wore knickers and caps. They were best friends. Fritz was the son of Moritz Pollak, a fashion and apparel wholesaler. He had received an excellent education in the best private school of Brno and graduated from Masaryk University. He knew how to present himself in front of women. Stela's eyes widened with surprise. She felt flattered to be on the side of such a smart-looking young man. Little did she know what was about to follow!"

Hilda continues. "Anita, the sky was a pale blue, a breeze smooth and perfectly crisp, you want to catch it in your hand. Everyone wore a smile. The temperature was exceptionally pleasant. The dress Stela wore was free flowing, below the knee, and revealed her svelte bodyline in a very discreet way. I put much love into that dress, Anita, in the same way I did for the headpiece she is going to wear at her wedding."

"How do you know all of that, Aunt Hilda?" I ask.

She looks at me with surprise, "Why do you ask?"

"I don't know," I said. "It seems as if you were there! Were you at the Sports Hall that Saturday?"

"I was. Darina and I decided to spy on the effect of what we had made!" She replied with a large smile and a mischievous look.

I did not know who Darina was. What I understood later is that Darina Dvorak helped with the dress. My aunt Hilda, an expert seamstress, loved making fresh, creative designs. Her beautiful sister, my mother, would wear Hilda's modern creations with gusto and pride at a fashion school she attended in Vienna.

Hilda sighs and finishes the story. "So your parents, Fritz and Stela, married the following year in 1925. They celebrated the event, close to the courthouse, at Hotel Barceló with their family and friends."

Anita's parents: Stela and Fritz (Bedřich) 1925
Photo Credit: Franze Grubner

CHAPTER 3

Pelikanova

I am attending school, and I can read and write. We live now on Pelikanova Ulice (Street) in a large square house at a crossroad going uphill to Špilberk Castle (German: Spielberg) that overlooks the town. It has a park where I play. The castle, built in the thirteenth century, holds much history. It sits on a hilltop near our home, where I spend the happy years of my childhood.

Many hundreds of years before my birth, in 1560, the town of Brno had bought the castle and made it into a municipal fortress.

My schoolteacher told us, "The bastion fortifications of the Špilberk castle helped the town defend itself against Swedish raids during the Thirty Years' War. That successful defense led to further fortification and the strengthening of the military function of the fortress.

"Three hundred years ago, after losing the Battle of White Mountain (*Bílá Hora*), the leading Moravian members of the anti-Habsburg insurrection lived, imprisoned, in Špilberk for several years.

"The battle marked the end of the Bohemian period of the Thirty Years' War."

With all this history behind us, I feel safe. My family has lived in this town ever since my grandfather Moritz moved here where he owned his business in wholesale apparel.

My parents and I live upstairs, and my grandparents live downstairs. My grandmother, Gisella, loves to read. Every day I see her reading her newspaper. She wears fashionable clothes and smells of spices. I relish her baked *kolá* (pies), those with apples or mushrooms and red cabbage. She has a quiet smile and often gives me wise advice. "Anita, you need to learn manners."

I run out of her apartment. Of course, I am a bit of a tomboy and do not care about manners. I am not fond of dolls either, nor knitting or sewing. I want to be a doctor, a surgeon.

My mother bakes delicious *plum dumplings* upstairs in our beautiful new kitchen. My father is away. He works hard. I do not see him often, except on Saturday, when we go to the club. We belong to a tennis association. He is teaching me to play, but it is only a few hours a week. I always look forward to the days we go. I wear a special tennis outfit.

***

In the deepest fold of my heart reside great memories of learning to play with my father. I cherish those memories of those few hours a week. He holds, at the time, the highest place in my heart.

***

We do not live far from the river named Svratka (Svra-tka), which meanders through town. A steamboat also goes to the lake, and we take it sometimes on Sunday with my grandparents, often stopping at castle *Veveň* built by Duke Conrad of Brno.

I live in a place surrounded by kings and queens and dukes as if I am their little princess. What could disturb the happiness of this place, this time?

Darina Dvorak is a friend of the family. She lives a few houses down. She and my mother are good friends. They speak German together. *Maminka* (mother) is very fluent in the language. She attended school in Vienna and consequently has an accent. I often make fun of it. She was born and raised in Břeclav (Brek-lav) a town on the Austrian and Slovakia border.

I am attending a secular school and enjoy learning. I learn easily and face no difficulty in school. I can bring home a B+ without trying too hard. My teachers also praise my attendance record.

Mrs. Vodka, our main teacher, is tall and relentless about our good behavior. Well, it is what we call her, but her name is Mrs. Vojtek.

My friend Ilse is sitting next to me. We are drawing a map of Europe. A boy sitting a few seats ahead has just sent me his latest secret message in his fountain pen *cloth-blotter* (A cloth-blotter is a piece of fabric to clean a fountain pen. Our mothers made one with several layers and a button holding those layers.)

When Mrs. Vodka is writing on the blackboard, I quickly pick it up. A piece of paper inside the blotter says, "Did you bring the sugar cubes?" I jot down an answer, "Yes," and slide the blotter back on the floor.

At recess, we go on with the plan, me running ahead with a pretend rope, and a long line of followers.

Mrs. Vodka's head is nodding in awe, and she smiles. I am popular with my school friends. I bring the sugar cubes for our game. I lead a herd of wild horses (mostly boys), and if they line up, I reward them with the sugar.

Soon the game will have to end. I see Mother's reserves of the sugar dwindling every time I sneak a handful into my pockets.

Me and my parents

Svestkove Knedliky

(Plum Dumpling)

2 eggs

2 cups of sifted flour (all-purpose)

2 cups of boiled potatoes, riced

1 cup of fine bread crumbs

12-15 plums

¼ cup cinnamon sugar

pinch of salt

2tbs butter

Cream 2 tablespoons of butter, beat in the eggs and salt. Gradually beat in the flour and riced potatoes. Knead the dough thoroughly.

On floured board, roll out dough to ¼ in. thick, then cut 3 inch squares. Lay 1 plum on each square, sprinkle with a little cinnamon sugar and fold edges over plum. Shape with hand in a ball. The wall of dough should be very thin. Drop dumplings into boiling salted water, cover and simmer for about 15 minutes. Brown bread crumbs, sprinkle with cinnamon sugar.

Made in our kitchen by Mother.

CHAPTER 4

Ilse

Me and my best friend Ilse.

I have a good friend. Her name is Ilse. She has no father. We are on the Maccabi soccer team together. She has light blonde hair and sparkly blue eyes. I enjoy playing with her. I love sports and it is the biggest part of our friendship.

However, our entrepreneurial personalities have us dreaming of other things. One day, Ilse and I decide to begin a business of our own in puppet making. We find our way to my aunt's shop. She always has a lot of colorful pieces lying on the floor.

With the permission of my aunt, we decide to create puppets made of leftover fabric and ribbons. Aunt Hilda helps us find strings to bring them alive. We find an amazing mix of ribbons and cloth made of various threads of textile, silk, cotton, and other materials, smelling of lemon and oranges. We sit for hours with our small scissors trying to create the best assembly of colors.

We also assist my aunt and enjoy seeing her customers and their new hats. We love trying them on, especially the wild and different ones Hilda makes for the opera house.

Hilda's Millinary's work

My aunt is busy making new designs every summer for the next opera season.

Often toward the end of the day, Hilda takes us to a coffee shop to have tea. What I like most about it is sitting there like grown-ups. People recognize Hilda and stop to talk with her, clients and handsome men. I am thinking:

"When I grow up, I am going to be like Aunt Hilda. I will go to coffee shops, but I am not sure about making hats. I am more inclined toward the medical profession."

Ilse and I bring our puppets to school, and friends beg us to make some for them.

My grandmother, Gisella (*babika*) takes us both to the Opera to see a performance of *Rusalka*. The mermaid in the story mesmerizes both. The colorful costumes made of gold over whites and reds are glorious. The singing and dancing is more than we had ever imagined possible.

For weeks we sing the "Song to the Moon":

"Svetlo tve daleko vidi

Po svete bloudis sirokem

Divas se v pribytky lidi.

Mesicku, postuj chvili

reckni mi, kde je muj mily "

Moon, high and deep in the sky.

Your light sees far,

You travel around the wide world

See into people's homes.

Moon, stand still a while

Tell me where is my dear.

The singer's voice is singing above our happy lives. We are both quite popular and are invited to many parties. I especially love those for Christmas, with all the lights on a tree with green needles and the shiny balls and funny characters hanging on the branches.

Ilse and I are seven and in our first year of school. Our enthusiasm for life has no bounds. Our friendship is very special. We are inseparable. My family will go to the Alps, near Austria and ski for the end of year holidays. I hope she will come with us.

CHAPTER 5

Aunt Lilly

"There is a thin line that separates laughter and pain,
comedy and tragedy, humor and hurt."

Erma Bombeck (1926–1996)

"**W**hy is it, *babičko* (grandmother), father does not have a sister? *Maminka* has a brother and a sister."

I wait for the answer, fidgety and embarrassed for my question. The answer seems slow to come. The wood floor is shiny and well polished. I stare at my leather shoes. They are made of fine blue pigskin. The white thread appears to weave in an interesting manner on the tip. My skirt is made of wool plaid and my stockings are matching and knitted with navy blue cotton.

My grandmother is looking preoccupied and silent. Her hair is neatly combed in a bun with a striking golden-brown braid. I see her back. She is not moving. Her checkered black-and-white apron is tied in a bow above the small of her back.

Perhaps, she did not hear my question. Taking a slow and deep breath, I bravely repeat it:

"Why is it, *babiko*, father does not..."

"...have a sister?" My grandmother continues.

Slowly, my grandmother turns toward me. Her face is still and grave, marked with tiny cracks around her deep hazelnut eyes. She takes me by the shoulder and points to a chair. She sits down. Both of her hands are on the table. She crosses her manicured fingers.

"Anita, he did, but we rather not remember. It is too painful. Her name was Lilly. She was a marvelous concert pianist. We had her attend the Brno Conservatory, as soon as it opened in 1919. Her career held so much promise."

Grandmother lets a long sigh, then continues:

"She even played in Vienna..."

"Oh! Really!" My brown eyes become large, the questions hanging on my eyelashes.

"Yes, sweetheart, it is a tragic story."

"Tragic?"

"Yes, everyone had told her not to, but she would not listen."

"You mean, like when I should stop eating your *paštika* (pate) or *koláč* (cake) but I don't hear you because it is so good!"

As soon as I finish my comment, remorse takes me over. Perhaps the comparison was not reasonable. I am young and have not known pain.

"Yes, something like that..." she continues. "He kept promising and she kept on believing. It was so very sad."

Suddenly, my grandmother becomes distant again, as if visiting lost memories. I can see the pain invading her face like a shadow of clouds moving on a beautiful day.

"Who was 'he'?" I reply with protective irritation in my voice.

"Well, she became infatuated with a professor at school. He was older. I think he had a hold on her ego. It was helpful because she excelled to please him. Nevertheless, when she came of age, he did not give her many chances to experience the world. He seduced her. Later, they married. He had a reputation of being a nefarious character, a

Casanova. It did not take long before he started seeing other women, this and that one. It broke her heart."

"So what happened?"

I hold my breath. Will Grandmother trust me with a secret? She can. I am almost eight now.

"Anita, she jumped off a bridge into the Svratka River."

It's as if a movie has suddenly stopped. My grandmother's face is frozen. Her eyes are staring as if she is reliving the fatality, but cannot bear the pain.
The water... the river... her dear child gone.
Tears are rolling down her cheeks. She pulls a crisp, white, embroidered handkerchief from her pocket. She dries her tears. I do not know what to say, but I stay with her. I feel confused. The grief my questions have brought up is horrifying to me.

This story confirms my ambitions to become a surgeon, rather than to pursue any other profession. How could one hold power over another? How could the control of another human being lead one to despair? On that day, I decide that I will never allow anyone to inflict that on me.

***

This is the first time I encounter loss and the effect of hurt and grief on someone. I never ask questions about Lilly again but search in my mind for a picture of my father's sister. I could put in that empty frame. She must have been a beautiful young woman. I imagined her flowing dark hair, her white and translucent skin, similar to the mermaid in Rusalka at the opera and playing at a grand black piano.

It is also the last time I hear of Lilly Pollakova. She had died before I came a long, but the secret possessed a special grip on me at that time. The realization that life is not always perfect and happy, that one can long for things or people one cannot have; the destructiveness of power and seduction.

CHAPTER 6

Michal

The Piano

Me and my brother, Michal
Photo: Franze Grubner

Frantisek Michal Pollak, born June 25, 1935.
This photo is standing on the piano in the dining room.

My brother's birth follows mine by five years. I now have to share a little. It does not always come easily, but I am old enough to feel that special bond between siblings, and especially the experience of the arrival of a baby in our family. He arrived June 25, 1935. His full name is Frantisek Michal Pollak.

Our home is decorated with modern furniture, whereas, my grandparents have "old furniture," what people call antique today.

Our sitting room has green furniture and a radio. In the dining room, there is a round table we elongate when guests visit and an imposing glass "vitrine" (a glass-paneled cabinet) on the right side. It holds my fascination. I can see teacups made of transparent porcelain laced with fancy motifs. My mother only opens it on special days, when she wears her white scalloped apron.

Every year on November 1st, a new elephant is added on my parents wedding anniversary, a new elephant is added. They are made of various materials—wood, glass, or porcelain—and looked at us as if they're saying, "I am looking over you guys. Don't you worry... no one can hurt you. We are here." Their peaceful presence is reassuring.

On the wall, at the left side of the table, there is a large painting that I am not supposed to touch. It says Paul Klee on the right. It has bright tones of reds and oranges. It is a lady looking at me.

Aside from our green and modern furniture, there are the Tugendhat chairs, also called Brno chairs, designed by Ludwig Mies, which are still rare.

However, people are talking about them as well as the Tugendhat House that is receiving its final coat of paint.

The day my brother arrives in our lives my grandparents are present. We are all gathered and seated on a green sofa. My brother is smiling, but also has just finished a feeding of my mother's milk. There is a strange and unique smell coming from him after his recent meal. As he smiles, the milk comes out at the corner of his mouth.

***

That was my brother; the scent of baby's milk and lactic acid and all of us adoring him.

***

My father loves music and has the voice of an opera singer. Music is part of my childhood every day. Habitually, we are gathered at the large dining table for a colorful and aromatic meal, often with visitors.

After dining we listen to someone who plays at the long concert piano.

We are allowed to stay with adults during these musical assemblies, but the music permeates the entire house. Michal, now three, plays with toys and listens attentively.

Last year, when I was seven, my parents sent me to the Conservatory to learn to play the piano. I am returning today from a lesson with the teacher. I place the sheet on the holder of the grand piano, where the harp is engraved in gold. Sitting on the bench I rehearse my music exercises. It is not a new one, but I am struggling with the notes. I did not do as well as I should have during my lesson. I want to make sure I can excel next time.

I sit down and start playing the music, over and again. Suddenly, I feel something on my side. Michal has climbed onto the bench next to me. His little hands are reaching for the keys. He starts playing the piece for me.

What happened on that day is something special that holds my love for my brother to this day, one of those magical moments that you always wonder if it truly happened. It remained our secret. He had an excellent musical ear. It was clear he would become a talented musician.

The memory of that moment still brightens every dark space of my present life. I feel his presence there helping me play those notes; helping me resolve whatever difficult task I try to carry out.

.

CHAPTER 7

My Aunt Hilda's Stories

"Brno"

Brno Opera, Mahen Theater

My Aunt Hilda begins:

"Let me tell you about another day Anita. It was a very special one you ought to know about." I love the way she tells me stories about "before," like the story about the day I was born, or when my parents met and how they got married.

"The day was May 26, 1928. It was the first day of the opening of the Exhibition of Contemporary Culture. The exhibition center is known today as BVV. On that day, the city of Brno gained the largest and most modern exhibition center in Central Europe.

"Your father, Fritz, wanted to show his father, Moritz, the new exhibit hall and had obtained tickets for everyone. Later, they were to meet Stela and his mother, Giselle, and go for dinner and then the opera.

"Annual markets and trade exhibitions have been held in Brno for 700 years, Hilda tells me. The city of Brno has a long-standing tradition of trade fairs. Our city becomes industrial, scientific, and logistics hub of central Europe. The booming textile industry within the city brought the first trade shows. People also need culture.

"Anita, we must go now, but I will continue the story later." Hilda brings me back home and leaves quickly. She must go and take care of a major client for the opera. They keep my aunt busy with costumes.

During other walks with my Aunt Hilda I learn that my grandfather, Moritz Pollak, is very active in directing his fashion business. He is very innovative—ahead of his time, Hilda says—most people still employ seamstresses. However, the "prêt-à-porter" (ready-to-wear) revolution is starting to take place, and Grandfather is at the forefront. My father is working in the sales end of the distribution. Wholesale merchants from Vienna, Linz, Saxony, Hungary, and Turkey attend annual markets in Brno.

The creation of Czechoslovak democracy took place ten years before today's event in Paris, the Czechoslovak National Council—signed by Masaryk, Štefánik, and Beneš—published the Czechoslovak declaration of independence. It was then proclaimed, ten days later, on October 28, 1918 in Praha. The Great War (WWI) is about to end and the Austro-Hungarian Empire about to collapse. Several ethnic groups and territories with different historical, political, and economic traditions blended and formed new state structures.

It is on these positive notes that the city of Brno starts to take shape. At the time of the declaration, the town had about 130,000 citizens. Among the population of Brno, 55,000 were German speakers, most of them Jewish. Brno Annual Exhibition Markets are regularly held. In the earlier years, the Brno city council decided on the project of a new international exhibition center. The construction lasted a year, and in 1928, the Brno Exhibition Centre was completed.

The Exhibition of Contemporary Culture represented a triumph for the Czechoslovak democracy. The phenomenal accomplishments of those ten years attested to the success of the new political approach. The town of Brno has been the capital of Moravia and part of Czechoslovakia for almost ten years now.

People from the town were looking forward to the day and were anxious to visit the important milestone. It was the inauguration of the Exhibition of Contemporary Culture in Czechoslovakia under the patronage of Tomáš G. Masaryk, the first President of Czechoslovakia.

It is why Aunt Hilda stiched yet another stunning outfit for my mother Stela. She puts a lot of love into the costume, the same way she did for all the others.

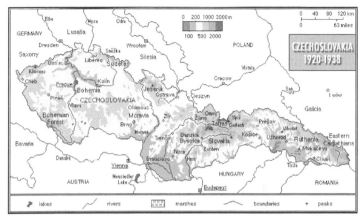

Moravia is the traditional region in central Europe, which served as the heart of a major medieval kingdom known as Great Moravia. Later, it was incorporated with the kingdom of Bohemia, and then the modern state of Czechoslovakia.

***

Over ten years ago, October 18, 1918 in Paris, the Czechoslovak National Council—signed by Masaryk, Štefánik, and Beneš—published the Czechoslovak declaration of independence. It was then proclaimed, ten days later, on October 28, in Praha. The newly created National Assembly assumed the first authority within Czechoslovakia on November 14, 1918.

It is on these good positive notes that the city of Brno starts to take shape. At the time of the declaration, the town had about 130,000 citizens. Among the population of Brno, 55,000 were German speakers, most of them Jewish. Brno Annual Exhibition Markets are regularly held. In the earlier years, the Brno town council decided on the project of a new international exhibition center. The construction lasted a year, and in 1928 the Brno Exhibition Centre was completed.

People from the town were looking forward to the day and were anxious to visit the important milestone. It was the inauguration of the Exhibition of Contemporary Culture in Czechoslovakia under the patronage of Tomáš G. Masaryk, the first President of Czechoslovakia.

***

It is why Aunt Hilda is sewing yet another stunning outfit for my mother, Stela. She put a lot of love into the costume, the same way she did for all the others.

CHAPTER 8

Hilda's Shop

with Darina Dvorak
Preparing for the
Exhibition of Contemporary Culture

Coco Chanel: Day ensemble, ca. 1927.

The Metropolitan Museum of Art. Costume Institute. 1984.31a–c

"*P*reparing for the Exhibition of Contemporary Culture before my birth. Here is what Darina remembered.

"What a superb fabric, Hilda! The best dress is yet to come. We are going to see Stela outshine every young married woman in Brno," exclaimed Darina Dvorak. "In view of the fact that she has a ring on her finger, we need to translate this into an outfit in accordance with the occasion."

Hilda replied, "Darina, we are never short of *idenngut* (good ideas) here, are we. Did you see what Coco presented at the last *schau* (show) in Paris? She wore a 'Day Ensemble': a dress with a shawl integrated over a pretty flower print made of silk chiffon, a low waist with a loose bow on it."

"Stela, I think I remember the look. I hear the dress also had hues of reds?"

"Yes, that's the one. Nothing *frevlerisch* (outrageous), close to the neckline...and slightly below the knee...a soft look, perfect for a daytime outfit."

"I understand this was not an easy cut. Coco Channel took the flowers from the pattern of the chiffon and apparently cut carefully to follow the floral pattern and used it for the neckline and the hem. This is a lot of work, Hilda!"

"It has fine pleats from the waist, in the front, to provide a little more opacity, I suppose.... The shawl is cut in the same manner as the hem.... I think I can do it. Why not? I am dating Heintz, and he is away a lot. It leaves me time at night. I want my little sister to wear the best. The dress is complex and so is the coat. I'll need to do the lining with the same approach... Oh! Let me get working on this. It is such an elegant outfit."

"Ach, I know you by now Hilda, nothing will faze you when it comes to your little sister. Let's get to it. Did you buy the fabric?"

"Yes."

"Oh, my word, it is beautiful. I can see it Hilda. I can."

From my aunt's words, I could imagine my parents, Fritz and Stela, together on that day, admiring the unique architecture of the building. It was, along with the elegant Villa Tugendhat, the most famous building from that period.

Ludwig Mies van der Rohe designed it. It was the modernist architecture of the time. It manifested the new identity of Czechoslovak society with the spirit of modern ideas and technological progress.

"Anita, I was present at that event too." My aunt Hilda covers the details of that day.

"Stela walked proudly by Fritz's side in the exhibit. Anita, she was mesmerized the first moment they met and remained by his side. She still felt the same today. This event reminded Stela of how they had met. The fairground with the Exhibition of Contemporary Culture was a turning point in Czech design and architecture. You need to understand, Anita, that this affair was representative of the existence of our independent country. Your grandfather Moritz was part of the movement along with others in 1905 to build Marsaryk University."

Reading about the history of the building and the architect, Fritz and Stela were strolling along the exhibit and learning about someone they had never heard of: The architect of this new building is Mies. He was born in Aachen, *Kingdom of Prussia.*

Further on, they read:

He worked in his father's stone carving shop, and at several local design firms before he moved to Berlin, where he joined the office of interior designer, Bruno Paul.

And later:

He began his architectural career as an apprentice at the studio of Peter Behrens from 1908 to 1912."

***

Fritz and Stela did not know just then, but I learned it at a later time. Mies would settle in Chicago, Illinois, where he would be head of the architecture school at Chicago's Armour Institute of Technology (later renamed Illinois Institute of Technology—IIT). Crown Hall is Mies' finest work, the definition of Miesian architecture. Later, along with Le Corbusier, Alvar Aalto, and Frank Lloyd Wright, he would be recognized as one of the pioneering masters of modern architecture. He created an influential twentieth-century architectural style, stated with extreme clarity and simplicity."

My hometown had more than enough to inspire anyone to succeed in this new phase of history.

***

Back to the present:

Hilda's face is rejoicing with the fond memories she is sharing.

"For this occasion Fritz and Stela, accompanied by your grandparents, Moritz and Gisella, were visiting the inauguration of an important landmark. The city planning and architecture were ranked among the highlights of European building culture of the twentieth century. The newly built exhibition grounds in Pisárky displayed an exhibition of science, education, and art as well as technical, economic, and additional branches of human activity. Anita, that was the most amazing exhibit I had ever seen. Our country was in full bloom, while America, as well as Germany, were going through a free fall."

***

In the city of Brno, modernism was to persist. Brno, the capital of Moravia and the Czech Republic's second-largest city, is a long way from Chicago. Brno was one of the hotbeds of innovation in central Europe. In America, the

International Herald Tribune was reporting on these new developments.

The years gave strength to the castle of my hometown, and the prosperity of the postwar era built confidence in my parents. Consequently, I enjoyed many good years full of comforts bought by my family's success.

I hold precious memories of ice skating, fun rendezvous with other girls my age, and holidays in the Austrian mountains during winter and summer. I loved where we lived; the old buildings with their red-tile roofs, and the many stores and bustled verve around us.

It was a lively town full of activities, such as markets on Saturdays and shops with beautiful things in windows. People seemed happy, and every casement had an abundance of flowers in the summer.

CHAPTER 9

Our Country

My Father, Fritz Pollak, and me.

I often see my father in uniform. He is a very active in the military and has a multicolor rank in the Czech Republic's army. By colorful, I mean that he has many colors on his uniform, but perhaps it is called a distinguished position. My mother says, "Your father is drafted." I am not sure what that means. Perhaps it is related to the insignia on his left breast pocket.

As a young man, he belonged to the Maccabi Club. The Club represented strong nationalistic views and supported youth sports with an emphasis on gymnastics and living in healthy ways.

Usually, I love listening to adults. Many of our friends often join my parents in the evening to listen to the radio together in the sitting room. No one speaks while they pay attention to the reporting.

No one shares with me the reasons for listening, and the announcer speaks too fast for me to understand. When a German speaks they lower the volume. It is, perhaps, due to his yelling. However, there is also a man who speaks English. He says things like:

"You have enemies? Good. That means you've stood up for something sometime in your life."

***

That was Winston Churchill.

***

In conversations between my father and grandfather, "Plzen" and "Skoda" are mentioned frequently. That is north of us, I understand, closer to Praha where my uncle lives with my other grandmother. They seem impressed by whatever was going on in Plzen. Later, I understand that it is a major manufacturing foundry important for the military. It makes guns and bullets for naval and land forces. Why is that so important?

However, that contributes some more to my sense of security. Everyone seems proud of it and the protection it must provide for our country.

President Tomáš Garrigue Masaryk's picture is in our school. Our teacher has told us that he was born in Brno. His parents could not read or write. He is an important person in our country. Thanks to him, we are now a republic as well as a democratic country. That means no Empire, no kings and queens. Well, then that means I have to relinquish my title as a princess? Not sure I like that.

Masaryk's parents were illiterate from Moravian Slovakia, yet he has done well. After grammar school in Brno, he attends the University of Vienna and was a student of well-known philosopher Franz Brentano. He later obtains a doctorate in Vienna and became a professor of philosophy at Prague University. He served in the Austrian Parliament and in the Young Czech Party.

Tomáš Garrigue Masaryk (1850–1937), President (1918–1935)

When the Great War (WWI) broke out in 1914, Masaryk concluded that the best course of action was to seek an independent country for Czechs and Slovaks. He realized, he could achieve his goals from outside the Austria-Hungary Empire.

***

At this time, Austria-Hungary is the world's great powers and geographically the second largest country in Europe after the Russian Empire.

The empire absorbed the region of Czech as well as Slovakia. Many conflicts caused the war. Imperialism versus nationalism was mostly at play. Therefore, Professor Masaryk left Prague, during the Great War and became a Professor of Slavic Research at King's College in London, lecturing on "The Problem of Small Nations". The reward of his efforts will subsequently secure his election as the president of our new nation.

***

Despite all these good steps, why are my parents and friends so interested in what the radio has to say? It's annoying to me. I want people to play the piano, not listen to the voice of some unknown person coming out of a box!

One day, I ventured into my grandfather's study while visiting with grandmother. Mother was away and grandmother was cooking in her kitchen.

On his beautiful wood desk with carving and locked drawers, I see a lot of newspapers' clippings, books and other papers. Besides the pictures of my grandmother Gisella and other people, I have not met. I see some documents neatly arranged. One page stands out, it has been read many times, but perhaps also crumpled and reopened again. Here is what it looks like:

Nuremburg Law. Issued 09-16-1935.

Inside this text, I read something very strange. The Nuremberg Laws say people with four German grandparents are "German or kindred blood," while people descending from three or four Judaic grandparents are

Jewish. Since when is nationality mixed with religious beliefs?

A person with one or two Jewish grandparents is a *Mischling*, that means a crossbreed, of "mixed blood." These are significant laws. This means that anyone considered Jewish by those standards will lose their citizenship.

What is this? Do they think we are dogs? Crossbreeds? Purebred or not, my shock is profound. What does it have to do with citizenship? So Cocker spaniels will become British and German Shepherds, German. The rest goes to a pound!

These laws, likewise, say that it is forbidden to have relations between "Jews" and non-Jewish Germans. It also prevents Jews from participating in German civic life.

I am so glad we do not live in Germany. What is this about? It is more than puzzling. It is horrifying! How could anyone come up with such laws? It is bloodcurdling.

Is it why my parents and their friends have a worried look on their faces? The lines on their faces are getting deeper every day. Now I get it.

My grandfather must be such a smart man. There are many books on his shelves. The backs are blue, red and gray with gold letters. Some are very old. Between books, I see sculptured animals and old tobacco boxes. On walls, frames with words like Honor, Proud etc... He must be so important.

Finally, after my thorough inspection, I decide to go to the kitchen to see if I could get some leftovers from *babika*'s delicious cooking. My grandfather is here, standing in the kitchen. He is wearing a suit, as usual, but his hands and arms are moving a lot. Usually, he is never home during the day. That's strange. He is telling a story to my grandmother. He seems upset and somber. I only catch the end of the story:

"...and they just shot them...they did that, Gisella. They weren't arrested, or anything else or taken to court..."

My grandmother's face looks horrified. She has a hand over her mouth. When she sees me, she comes over and takes me by the shoulders and hugs me in front of her, facing my grandfather Moritz, as if to protect herself from what he had just said. From her embrace, I look up to my grandmother and say, "What is it *babika*? What is it?"
She is staring at my grandfather. Her mouth is moving but no sound is coming out. My grandfather leaves quickly.

"My sweet child, your grandfather and I were just having a discussion."

"He said they just shot them...who was it?"

"Oh, it was just in the news. Some people broke down windows of the shop owners. They were upset..."

"Did they do this here?"

"No, sweetheart, not here but in Germany, far away...it could never happen here, don't worry."

She gives me a big hug and sent me on my way back upstairs to my parents.

***

Looking back, I now realize my grandparents were discussing that day the event of Kristallnacht. One of the areas affected was the Sudetenland. The area, where my mother, aunt, and uncle were born; Sudentenland encompassed

CHAPTER 10

Changes

My Grandfather: Moritz Pollak

I turned nine a few months ago. Leaves are almost all gone; yellow and red hues are slowly disappearing. Something strange has happened. Things are starting to change. People in gray uniforms have moved into town. We have to follow new rules. I no longer attend school. Consequently, I am spending a lot of time behind windows looking out. I see the road to the castle on the hill and there is always activity.

Our castle is now home to a new king. His name is *Germon*; I think. I hear the name everywhere! A new flag on the castle has replaced the old one with the blue triangle and the two red and white stripes. I see a lot of trucks going up the road with that insignia. It is a white circle on a red background and a bizarre black cross. Since father has been in the military, he believes they will consider him for his title of officer in the Czech army.

As these changes occur in town, there are lots going on, and I can't quite follow why and what they are all about. Is this relating to this new law?
Why is the arrival of a fresh king causing all this turmoil and tension? Should we not be happier? I am confused. I

thought we didn't want Kings and Queens anymore. Today, we hear the sound of horns playing music outside.

"What is going on, Mother? Are we going to get a queen too?"

"*Schatzi* (darling), it isn't about a queen, unfortunately. It is about Hitler."

"Hitler? What does he have to do with our town? Our teacher says he lives in Berlin, as the president of France, Lebrun, lives in Paris!"

"Yes, my sweet, and Franklin Roosevelt lives in Washington, and presides over the United States; you are right they should stay in their country, but the chancellor of Germany has a different idea. He wants to add all of us to his side. First, the *Anschluss* (annexation of Austria)...."

"What a 'hoodwink!' But, can it benefit us?"

"I'm not sure I can answer the question, *hloupý* (silly)! I agree. We were happy where we were, a new republic, good presidents, first President Masaryk then Edvard Beneš came along. He had to resign and Emil Hácha, we fear, is a puppet of the German government."

"Beneš? I heard *tatinek* (father) say he is away in England. I am not sure what he is doing in London now!"

"London? I wish we were in London! Do you want to hear the latest, *schatzi*?" she asks, suddenly serious.

"Y...yes?" I answer with hesitation.

"Your father has to turn over our home to officers. Since we live down from the castle, we are a convenient place for their offices."

"Isn't the castle big enough?" I ask my mother with anger.

"*Schatzi,* it isn't so, unfortunately. It is about him. Hitler."

"Hitler, Hitler," I stomped around the kitchen. "This man has me aggravated. Who is he? Who does he think he is? What a portentous, pompous, plastered down pompadour *yobo* (bully)!

"I wish I could tell you what is in this man's head, Anita. He is a madman for sure. The worst is something you need to understand. He holds these sick beliefs about people of Jewish descent. He has a theory and a widespread propaganda about us, that we carry familial diseases in our genes."

"Is this for real? I read about the new Nuremberg laws, but..."

"...so he feels that anyone with this genetic inheritance is inferior because of it."

"Inferior! Again, what is his beef?" I am furious at the idea that people treat us differently. What will happen next?

"But they say, there is a solution. We will move out of town and then we will see."

This conversation has me fuming. First, no school, now our move... I decide to share my feelings with the pompous king.

Initially, I go to the piano and hit keys loud and in a cacophony. Later I decide to go to my room and armed with a fountain pen and piece of paper, I start writing.

Dear Mr. Adolf Hitler:

I am nine years old and I just found out that I am no longer allowed in school. Could you please explain?

One day, my teacher tells us why school is obligatory and that everyone needs to receive an education. The next day I am no longer allowed in class. I do not carry any diseases. Why are my friends avoiding me, what did you tell them?

I also would like to share that our family is not pleased about all these changes. We have to give up our home for your officers, and then my father is unable to do his regular work and is now a chauffeur! What a waste of his talents!

Please send a response at once,

Anita

I fold the letter and put it in an envelope. I write on an envelope:

Hitler of Berlin, Germany
Špilberk Castle

When my father returns from work, I hand it to him. He looks at me with a question wrinkling his forehead. I refuse to explain and walk to my room.

I marched back to my room as if going to the next state council meeting.

***

I am not sure the letter was ever sent, but even if it was, I doubt Herr Führer had time for little girls' letters. One thing I know, I was on the path to a mission. Had the man looked at himself? He certainly did not have blond hair and blue eyes!

Hitler was busy convincing the Germans who lived on the borders of Czechoslovakia to revolt against our country. Hence, the infamous Munich Agreement was signed the prior year on September 30, 1938.

A few days later, Hitler again entered the Sudetenland and visited the famous spa town of Karlsbad (Karlovy Vary), greeted by Sudeten Germans.

For Hitler, the Munich Agreement was nothing more than a worthless piece of paper. On October 21, just three weeks after signing the document, he informed his generals that they should begin planning for "the liquidation of the remainder of Czechoslovakia," a clear violation of the agreement.

Hitler promised British Prime Minister Neville Chamberlain, and the German people; the Sudetenland would be his "last territorial demand" in Europe. In reality, it was only the beginning. And Hitler now wanted to grab the remainder of Czechoslovakia because of its strategic importance.

By now, the Nazis perfected the art of stealing neighboring territory. They would start by encouraging political unrest inside the area. At the same time, they would wage a propaganda campaign citing real or imagined wrongs committed against local Germans.

When neighboring political leaders finally came to see Hitler in order to resolve the ongoing crisis, they would be offered help in the form of a German Army occupation to "restore order."

President Eduard Beneš had fled to England after the Munich Agreement fearing assassination by the Nazis.

The new political leader of Czechoslovakia was 66-year-old Dr. Emil Hácha, an inexperienced politician with a bad heart condition. Czech Hácha now presided over an ever-shrinking republic. By early 1939, two outlying border areas were seized by Poland and Hungary with Hitler's approval.

Now, all that remained of shrunken Czechoslovakia were the two central provinces of Bohemia and Moravia. At this point, Goebbels' propaganda machine went into high gear, spreading reports of alleged persecution of local Germans by Czechs.

***

Reluctantly, we move outside of the city into a smaller place. My grandparents are with us as well.

My father is now relegated to serving officers. All these people with gray uniforms and breast pockets on their jackets are full of colors. They also wear caps with visors and more colors on them. My *tatinek* only gets to wear a black visor. He is mad. He says, "Why me? I did not do anything wrong! You would think our government would stand for me. But no, I am an alien now."

"An alien?" I look at him. "What's that?"

"Someone without status or rights in his country" he answers.

"How could that be?" I have heard of our rights as citizens in school, and now someone was taking those away. Finally, I put it together. What I read at my grandfather's desk...that's it. I get it. I am shaking inside, realizing what this means for all of us.

Since my school dismissal, my friends are refusing to speak to me. In addition, we have to display an insignia on our clothes, which is a yellow star. If we don't, we could be shot on the spot, just what my grandfather had said to my grandmother.

Friends and strangers alike look the other way when we walk on the street. I hate this. What reasons do these people in gray uniforms have to take over our castle, disturb our peace, and decide that we should be outcasts? There isn't a day that I am not bullied, teased by some of the other kids. I don't want to go out anymore.

People are talking about: "Kindertransport." My parents want me to go. I point blank refuse to go anywhere without them. I lock myself in the bedroom to make a point. What would I do, take a train with all these other kids to go to Switzerland? Eat chocolate while they are here without me!

My grandparents are also very upset. My grandfather, who is tall and thin and wears a mustache, is usually calm and contained. However, what I call his "whiskers" are moving a lot lately.

One day, my grandfather goes to town for a meeting. He is walking on the road coming back when a cyclist rides by and hits him accidentally. The cyclist seems badly injured, so grandpa brings him to the hospital. The cyclist improved and left the hospital. They kept my grandfather for concussions. A few weeks later, he died of pneumonia.

My grandmother, *babička,* is in pieces. She sheds tears that could fill our bathtub. There is much to cry about these days. Sorrow fills our small apartment. The old gray wall without pictures does not feel like home, and a tiny kitchen where we all squeeze in at night for an evening meal needs a lot of repairs. I now sleep with my grandmother at night. I don't want my mother to see her without teeth.

Needless to say, our family is broken and disordered by all these changes. The dominos can't be *kyboshed* (stopped).

CHAPTER 11

A League of Nations

A commemorative card depicting President of the United States,
Woodrow Wilson, and the "Origin of the League of Nations."

I am at home most of the time, in a small apartment we all share, but still eager to learn. Without school, days are long. I look around for things to fill time.

My attention falls on the Great War and the formation of the "League of Nations." Woodrow Wilson was behind this idea. He was the President of the United States. His first office was in London, and then it was moved to a neutral country, Switzerland. The new idea was to bring peace between nations.

President Wilson had enthusiastically promoted the idea of the League as a means of avoiding any repetition of the bloodshed of the Great War, and the creation of the League was a centerpiece of Wilson's Fourteen Points for Peace.

I read the following: In 1919, the Nobel Peace Price is awarded to Woodrow Wilson for his peacemaking efforts. He inspired independence movements around the world.

What is the League of Nations? I am very intrigued now. I look in an encyclopedia and read:

"The League of Nations is an intergovernmental organization founded as a result of the Paris Peace Conference that ended the Great War."

That's the war my grandfather mentioned. (Today we call it World War I.) I continue reading: "It is the first worlwide organization whose principal mission is to maintain world peace. Its primary goals, as stated in its Covenant, included preventing wars through collective security and disarmament, and settling international disputes through negotiation and arbitration."

It all sounds good, so? "Other issues in it and related treaties include labor conditions, just treatment of native inhabitants...and protection of minorities in Europe."

I breathe a large sigh; protection of minorities! So if we are a minority...my mind is busy processing this idea. Eventually, feeling triumphant after I read this, I realize that this means perhaps there is protection for us?

At dinnertime, we are all sitting around the kitchen table with my grandmother, and I announce my discoveries.

"Have you heard of the League of Nations?" I venture. "It seems like a pretty good idea." I continue after a long pause.

A delicious soup, steaming in the serving bowl, is passed around.

"Well, Anita," my father finally says. "The 'big guys' can write laws and conventions, make points and agreements. However, these are not always followed, and it means more war and more fighting. Then we had the Kellogg-Briand Pact or Treaty of 1928 that outlawed war."

"Oh, but *tatinek*, aren't we organized to stand up to these problems?"

"Yes, we are. A lot of efforts were expanded since the last war in creating a sense of nationalism. For example, I attended the Maccabi Club, and we live in a republic now. Nevertheless, democracies are fragile...before, we lived in a monarchy."

"What is a monarchy, *tatinek*?"

My father does not answer. He is absorbed in reading the newspaper on the table. His eyebrows are close together, which is usually not a good sign.

All these big words, the Kellogg-Briand Pact? What is that? I need to check into it. That sounds interesting.

Later in my reading, I discover that the "Kellogg-Briand Pact is an agreement to promise not to use war to resolve disputes or conflicts of whatever nature or of whatever origin they may be, which may arise among them.

Ten years ago this pact was signed. It is also called the Pact of Paris, for the city where it was signed and sponsored by France. The pact was one of many international efforts to prevent another war." So why is everyone talking about war? I miss my piano. How can such insanity be going on and no place to express it in notes? I am not a happy girl.

***

Of course, what I did not know then was that the Versailles Treaty was a vindictive peace. Mostly imposed by the Frenchman named Daladier. Wilson had to bend on many of the Fourteen Points to get the League. Germany was assigned all culpability for that Great War (WWI). The guilt clause was used by Hitler to stir up nationalism, and that can be very dangerous when taken to extremes.

CHAPTER 12

Another Change

My grandmother *Babička*: Gisella Pollak

We have finally settled down in our new small place outside of town, when a new order comes requesting all Judaic families to move to this new town. It will be a safe town for us because the Jewish Council will protect us.

Things cannot be worse. These days our lives look as if shadowed by the darkest black clouds. I understand that our country is no longer a republic but a "Protectorate." In other words, we are under German protection. I wonder what kind of protection this is, having us move and taking us out of jobs and schools?

My father says:

"They might think we are poor schlimazels (unlucky people), but not again. We'll see who wins! Let's pack again."

Still, I cannot understand what the "big deal" is about us Jewish families. First, we are not homeless. My parents appeared to be able to give us more than most of my girlfriends back in school. We rarely attend a synagogue, so what does this religion of my ancestors have to do with us? Why are we differentiated among all the others in town?

Everyone had bowed to my grandfather before this nonsense began. He was a distinguished gentleman, as was my father.

Babika spills all these tears because we have to move again. One day, she stops crying and talking and just stares a lot. It lasts weeks, but there is so much going on, in a way it is better than her torrential outpours.

But it comes to a head. One day, in the morning, my mother calls me. Her face is very red as if she has cried. She says.

"Anita, schatzi (darling), Grandma has joined Grandpa."

"Oh!" My eyes open wide, "What do you mean, Mother?"

"Just what I said. She left us."

My mother's apron is all wet, and she is wiping lots of tears from her eyes.

"But how? I don't understand, did she go away to Praha?"

"No, not that way, *schatzi*. She left for good."

"But *maminko*, how could she? You mean died? But she was never in the hospital. Isn't it the way people leave for good?"

"Not always..." She hesitates, "Some people choose to die."

Gradually, I remember Lilly. The family secret and the pain I had seen on my grandmother's face that day.

"Do you mean like...jump in the river like Aunt Lilly, because of her sorrow?" I frown and look at *Maminka*. My heart is sinking slowly with the thought of the disappearance of my beloved *Babika*.

"Yes, it is what I mean. She did not wake up."

"Is this what people mean by: '*Liebesleid*' (dying of grief)?" I ask.

Mother is quiet, and tears well up again in her eyes. She removes her apron soaked in tears.

"Please, I never want to hear German spoken again."

"*Maminko*...." My heart is feeling blurry, and I squeeze her with all my might. Her shoulders are shaking as she holds her tears, trying not to cry in front of me. Her face is swollen, cherry-colored and changed. The small gray kitchen where we stand huddled together is shrinking and appears oddly shaped. The world feels as if it is spinning.

"Mom, *Maminko*." I say, "everything will be all right, Papa said so. It will be."

She finally takes hold of her emotions and gets up from the frayed rattan chair.

"Where is your *bratr* (brother) Michal?"

"Mom, I will find him," I get up eagerly to help and look for him. I find him playing quietly in another room with his lead soldiers.

"Look Anita!" His eyes are wide open and show excitement.

He shows me a box that is our castle and the soldiers who are my father's troop defending our castle.

"Now, we won this time. We send them all home, the soldiers from Germany!"

I smile at his hopefulness. He has a big smile on his face, and some left-over chocolate mark on around his plump lips. I don't have the courage to tell him about Babika and that her chocolate favors will no longer be.

Back in the kitchen, mother seems calmer. I asked her: "*Maminka*, I remember one day when Grandfather came home very upset and Grandmother became upset as well after he spoke to her. He was saying something like... and they shot them, right there... What do you think that was about?"

"I think I remember that day, Anita. Well, a few years ago now, something happened in Paris. A young man was upset and killed someone. Soon after, something horrible happened. People broke into window shops of every store owned by Jewish businessmen, every synagogue, and every school. That is what they call the Night of Crystal (Kristallnacht)."

"Oh, no. Nice name, but... what a horrible thing!" I looked at her in disbelief. "Why? Why would they do something so horrible?"

"I know, my love. It is hard to believe so much hatred is possible."

"I know." I stare at my bitten nails. Angst is ravaging me inside.

The hole my grandparents are leaving behind is unbearable. That night, I could not go to sleep. I stared into the darkness for a very long time. Could this be possible? Why would people hate us so much? What have we done?

CHAPTER 13

Anger

Photo taken in 1937.

My letter to Mr. Hitler was not answered. I feel so upset. I decide to take my soccer ball downstairs on the porch of the old brick house. Down below our new apartment a few small stores are selling fresh food and baked goods. It is noon. I look around no one is out. Stores are closed. Merchants are back home having lunch with their families. I have winter shoes on with heavy soles because snow is on the ground. As I walk around, stomping in frustration, a light comes through my mind. I approach an open area.

I look back still no one is here. With all the force of my right boot, I kick a soccer ball. A few seconds later, I hear broken glass. I look at what I just did with horror. The soccer ball had crossed the road and, with all its force, had hit a small window in the basement floor of a store. I did not expect the results to be as striking. I stare at the broken window in disbelief.

Slowly, I walk away as if nothing happened. I feel better, but now I am embarrassed. The storeowner is a nice man and did not cause *babika* to die. What got into me? I walk back upstairs, holding my head down. I do not discuss with my mother what just happened.

No one knew of the incident. I was never punished for my small mischief. It remained my secret.

I understood later, my grandmother had ended her suffering with a cup of pills. It is when I learned that grief could turn on you if you don't address it. We never had a funeral for her, or for my grandfather; there was no time.

Aunt Hilda and Uncle Heintz visit a lot now. He travels regularly and knows what is going on. Whatever it is, it must be bad. He has lost his smile and sparkles are no longer in his eyes. I never hear of details, but I know they talk late at night—my parents with my uncle and my aunt. The strangled explosion of Hilda's feelings comes through their whispers.

"Oh mmm, ah mmm."

Hilda is a strong, modern woman. For her to make all these sounds must not be good. That's what I think as I am struggling to fall into a barren child sleep. Innocence is fast slipping into the ravine of the war.

***

Naturally, I was angered by all these changes. We only had heard of some particulars, such as Beneš leaving,

Hácha being sworn as President. He was older and perceived to be on the side of Germany. We did not know how it all had happened. Our new fragile president bullied into surrender.

It is what we understand today. Our president was unnerved by some of the events in Czechoslovakia. He sent a message to Hitler requesting for a face-to-face meeting to resolve the ongoing crisis. Hitler, of course, agreed to see him as soon as possible.

The president was unable to fly, due to his heart condition, and arrived by train in Berlin on a Tuesday evening. He was met by Foreign Minister, Ribbentrop, and taken to the Adlon Hotel to await Hitler's call.

Nearly three hours later, at 1:15 AM, Hácha was finally summoned to the Reich Chancellery to see the Führer. At this meeting, Hitler let our president speak first and for as long as he wanted. President Hácha proceeded to humble himself unabashedly in the presence of the all-powerful German dictator.

He disavowed any link with the previous democratic government of Czechoslovakia and promised to work toward eliminating any anti-German sentiment among his people. He then pleaded for mercy on behalf of his little country.

Hácha's pitiful pleading and groveling brought out the worst in Hitler. He had utter contempt for human weakness. When Hácha finished his monologue, Hitler launched into a blistering attack, citing all of the alleged wrongs committed by Czechs against Germans.

Working himself into a state of rage, Hitler hollered out that his patience with Czechoslovakia had ended, and that the German Army was to invade the country, beginning in just a few hours.

"Now," the Führer bellowed, his face red and his fists clenched. "The Czech people have two options. Offer futile resistance and be violently crushed, or you can sign a document telling your countrymen to receive peacefully the incoming troops."

Our president had to decide soon. The troops would march in beginning at 6 A.M. President Hácha just sat in disbelief. He was taken completely by surprise and was too shocked to respond.

Hitler was done with him for the time being and sent him into an adjoining room for further discussions with Hermann Göring and Foreign Minister Ribbentrop. As he was asked to return to the first room, they immediately pounced on the sickly president, badgering him to sign the surrender document, placed on the table before him.

Our president refused to sign outright. They insisted again, even pushing a pen at him. He refused once more. Then Göring, in a final resort, played his trump card. He told our president, that unless he signed, half of Prague would be bombed to ruins within two hours by the German Air Force (Luftwaffe). When he heard this, our frail president collapsed onto the floor.

The two men panicked, thinking they had killed the man with fright. Dr. Morell, Hitler's personal physician, was rushed in, and he injected the president with vitamins and who know what else to revive him.

When Hácha recovered his senses, the Nazis stuck a telephone in his hands, connecting him with his government back in Prague. Hácha spoke into the telephone and reluctantly advised his government to surrender peacefully to the Nazis.

As Czechs were enraged by what was going on, apparently so were the prior president, Beneš, and his followers. The Czech resistance network that existed during the early years of the WWII operated under the leadership of the former Czechoslovak president Edvard Beneš. Together with the head of Czechoslovak military intelligence, František Moravec, he coordinated resistance activity while in exile in London. Its long-term purpose was to serve as a shadow government until Czechoslovakia's liberation from Nazi's occupation.

***

Uncle Heintz is back from another trip. He and Hilda are visiting. He talks about how difficult and dangerous it is to travel these days. Hilda seems nervous. The joyous meals we usually share are replaced by long silences. Anxiety of the unknown hangs in the air like a ghost. Michal keeps a monologue of stories going. Adults are frozen in fear. Nevertheless, he feels the need to disperse the silent clouds that have invaded the kitchen where we are all sitting.

Our minds invaded gradually with hopelessness and uncertainty, we sit, pressed against each other at the small table. Michal has left the room to play with his soldiers. A loose fly is searching for something. The sound from the movement of its wings is the only noise, except for the tick-tock of the clock on the kitchen wall. Angst is hovering over us. It has moved in with us for good, as a new invisible resident of our very tiny apartment.

CHAPTER 14

Games

Czech Marionette

I am now eleven. It's the number on the clock, closest to noon, I told my brother. He is learning to count. We moved here when he was only four. So he has never attended school. I try to teach him what I had learned in school. Now our time is spent mostly together. One day, he asks:

"How is it one rides a bicycle?"

He heard of the accident from my grandfather. We did not have a bicycle anymore, so I try to think of how I could explain. I had spent many happy hours on a red tricycle in our old home was given away. We could not keep it.

"Take this chair Michal, sit on it with the back in front."

Michal goes to get a small chair and sits as instructed.

"Now hold the front. Here is your handlebar."

"So?" He is looking at me, six years worth of questions engraved in his eyes.

Marion A. Stahl

"Well, now imagine you have a hoop and tires in front and back of the chairs. Under your feet are pedals, and you push to make the wheels move forward."

"Really, is that's all?"

"Well, of course, a few other details. Michal, it has to be all attached together, so it moves forward."

"I get it. I think in one of my books, I saw something resembling it."

He is holding onto the back of the chair and dangling his little legs in a circular motion. The chair cracks, unaccustomed to this new use. Michal continues on his bicycle for hours, pretending to be riding in a park or going places. He often seems to be living in an imaginary world of his own.

Michal barely knows how to read, and relies on images to learn. I have found a way to live without the piano. I sit at a table and pretend. I draw the keys on a piece of paper, and I sing the notes. When will we get it back? I miss the evening musical gathering with friends.

We play with a puppet theater that belonged to my grandparents and invent stories. The tale is of two young people going to live in a new town. Our puppets have faces made of wood and strings. Ma, my mother's mother, bought them for us when we went to Praha to see my cousins a few years ago. I liked that town. We had loads of fun. We had never laughed so much. My brother and I rode on horses on a carousel. We ate things on the square. An old man was playing the saxophone and we danced. Store windows displayed puppets. I wanted them all, but I held my desire in check this time.

Once, when I was younger, I had a row with my father. I was a little horror then. My brother wasn't born yet. I was showered with many gifts, being the only grandchild at that time. We were walking on the street of my early years, Orli Street. The street had many shops. Our building was very new and had a glass and crystal shop. I loved window-shopping and admiring all the beautiful objects that could be bought. When we arrived at a toy store, I pointed at a toy I wanted. My father said, "No, Anita, you have enough toys."

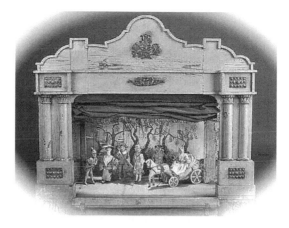

It was not the answer I wanted. Therefore, I continued with pig-headed insistence:

"No, I want this! I have to have it." Suddenly, I saw my father's eyes grow wide, and his face turn red. He grabbed me by the collar and lifted me in the air.

"No, I said no, Anita. If you do not stop, you will stay in the air. Do you understand?"

Naturally, suspended in the air, facing my father's angry grimace wasn't going to be any fun. I began to cry, and he let me back down on the ground. I continued to cry from the reprimand, but got the lesson imprinted in my head. That attitude wasn't going to work with him.

***

Czechoslovakia has an important tradition with Puppet Theater. As a medium for political messages, it enjoyed greater freedom than its counterparts in "legitimate" theater, opera, and dance. The Hapsburgs, the Germans, and later the Soviets, underestimated its relevance and potency. During this time, Czechoslovakia's Puppet Theater was a hotbed of national resistance. It was childlike and performed in a foreign language. Eventually, the Germans noticed one overbearing puppet character meant to recall Adolf Hitler and arrested that troupe's leader as well as some of the puppets.

***

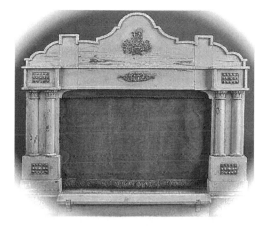

Our play with the puppets is over. I hear a sound of someone in the next room. Mother is preparing to cook a *Makovy Kolac*. It is my favorite.

Maminka first breaks and separates the eggs into two containers: the yellow in one and the transparent jelly in another. I love the aroma of the brown powder, the lemon. It reminds me of family celebrations. When she adds the black poppy seeds and the white sugar to the bowl, it looks like fine coal powder and snow. She makes more puffy snow with the jelly from those eggs. I am sitting at the head of the table on a stool. She lets me stir the preparation and lick what is left on the mixing spoon.

Makovy Koláč

(Poppy-Seed Layer Torte)

1 cup of sugar

6 eggs, separated

1 cup of ground poppy seeds

1 cup of heavy cream, whipped

¼ cup of raisins, plumped

½ teaspoon of ground cinnamon

¼ teaspoon each of ground cloves and mace

½ cup of apricot, strawberry, or raspberry jam

Grated ring of lemon

Cream butter, add sugar, and beat in egg yolks. Stir in remaining ingredients (except jam and cream.) Beat egg whites. Fold in batter. Grease and flour two 9-inch layer cakes pans. Spoon half of batter into each. Bake in oven (350f) for 3(minutes. Fill cold layers with jam. Top with whipped cream.

From *Maminka's* kitchen.

CHAPTER 15

"Aufruf"

Evacuation order, written by the Jewish Council.

*T*rees are blossoming as we prepare for this new move. Our belongings are reduced yet again. We can only bring one valise each. Outside, I can see from our window, there are continuous activities for the preparation of other families leaving. There isn't a day where we do not see a family leaving, suitcase in hand. Where are they going? I wonder. It isn't yet time for the transport to the town. Usually, it is dark when they depart.

I hide behind the handmade lace curtains my grandmother hung on the windows.

During this period, my uncle leaves us too. He has seen more than we all knew and also decided to end his life. When she comes over, Hilda tells us, between long sobs, "I found him next to the oven..." she is holding his note:

"I can't imagine going to live in this town and wait for them to take me, please forgive me."

The police come to take his body, and Hilda goes with them.

We are busy with our imminent departure. We wanted to believe she is in a safe place. We are distributing our last belongings among trusted friends. My father had moved our beloved and beautiful grand piano to a storage house during our first move.

Mr. Henry Steinway Senior would have rolled in his coffin if he knew where one of his pianos slept! I know how proud my parents were of the acquisition coming from America.

Now our small suitcases are ready for a new destination. The town is north of Praha. My brother and I are now inseparable. We realize a thousand things occupy our parents' thoughts. We put on our best clothes, so they will not take too much space in our suitcases.

Michal asks:

"Anita, do you think I should take my Poky with me?" Poky is my brother's bear. He has been inseparable from his dear companion since our last move.

"I don't know, but I think you would be better taking him along. He'll be safe with you."

Dolls have never been important to me, since I have my brother. I look through the small space containing my special belongings. I choose to take a chain my grandmother gave me.

"OK then, Poky, you are coming along." I hear my brother say in the background. For a second, I expect his bear to formulate a grunt or a real answer. He has been so much a part of our lives in this past year that he is alive in my head too.

Friends of our family have decided to take a different route. They are going to escape to Switzerland. Others are going to stay with family in northern countries closer to Russia. From there, they are planning to ask for asylum in America. My father is not pleased about it. He feels that he has served his country and isn't going to abandon it. Surely, the war is going to be over soon, and all will return to normal.

Today, he is wearing khakis and a crisp striped shirt. On his head, his once thick wavy hair is getting thinner by the day. He is explaining to his friends his convictions. His face is tense, and I see his pain.

"Yes...no...no..." I do not hear the conversation, but I can see by the motion of his head, In addition, his arms are waving through the air. He is downstairs, speaking to someone on the street.

My mother says, "He is a passionate man and strong in his beliefs."

Could it get us exempted from moving again? However, despite all his efforts and the admiration I have for my father, he is not able to change the course of our destiny.

As if we are going to an important event, the four of us leave the house neatly dressed, each with a small suitcase. I hold Michal's hand, and my father my mother's hand. Not a word is exchanged. We walk to the site where the train is waiting for us.

In my memory, I can still see the train we took to the Austrian mountains to go skiing. The train compartments had windows and seats covered with a beautiful fabric. The smoke from the steam locomotive...

I heard that we are going to the *Umschlagplatz*, but I do not dare to use the word in front of my mother, since it is in German. We call it: *Překládky*, (transshipment). My tatinek purchased tickets for the trip.

Other families are going in the same direction, walking fast as if fleeing an invisible enemy. Most faces are grave, unsure of the future.

Their dark silhouettes shadowed on the mustard colored limestone houses. What is tomorrow going to bring? I look forward to the train ride, but detest the unsettling feeling of all that is unknown. I miss going to school, having parties with girlfriends, attending gym classes, and playing tennis with my father. Is it what war is about, deprivation? My brother is still so fresh and full of hope. His voice is singing in my ear like a pleasant melody, "Anita! Will there be ice cream where we're going? Will we still be able to read books at night together?"

"I don't know, Michal. I certainly hope so." However, deep inside, doubts are slowly invading me.

"Anita! Where are Grandpa, Grandma, Aunt Hilda and Uncle Heinz? Are they not coming along? Will we see them again?" His eyes are so insistent and full of hope. I do not have the courage to answer truthfully.

"I hope we will. I miss them too, you know."

The street fills with the rhythmic sound of our leather shoes, the metal tips resonating on the pavers. The silence of our voices is oppressive. I start singing a song Grandmother taught me. I don't remember all the words, but the humming is keeping me focused.

We arrive at my former school on Merhautova Street not far from the train. We are to meet there with others and wait. When we arrive at the station, things are a bit different than I had imagined.

First, we are given tags to put around our necks. Then, there are no windows in the train compartment. Next, no seats; we are sitting on our suitcases. There are so many people.

We are pushed around. Michal is crying. My parents are standing rigid with anger and fear. Feelings are growing in me too. Where are we going? Did my uncle know?

***

At that time, the Jewish population in Brno was 11,102. Over 10,000 Jews were deported to Terezín in thirteen transports. The very first transport departed for Minsk in November 1941; the last one headed for Terezín, in June 1943.

The day of our transport was March 23, 1943. My family was on the transport called "Ad". The point of departure was my elementary school on Merhautova Street, where a memorial plaque can be seen on the house today. A mere 700 survived the journey.

It was the last time I ever heard from Hilda. No one knows what happened to her.

Marion A. Stahl

CHAPTER 16

Paradise Town

Drawing by children in Paradise Town

*T*his trip feels unending. The compartment smells of urine, and I finally decide to put my head on my mother's knees and fall asleep to forget what is happening to us. A voice awakens me some time later.

"Two hundred and fifty kilometers," another person continues from somewhere in the train car, "north of Praha."

"Isn't someone going to bring us food and at least water?" a lady pleads.

No response comes, only the rhythmic sound of the metal wheels against the track. My parents are dead to the world. While I was snoozing, I dreamt; I was playing the piano. The notes were strangely monotonous and had lost their melodious tone. The rest of the ride is buried in the pain of hunger and thirst, horrible smells, sounds of babies crying. It is dark inside the train. Will our future be as dark?

The night is falling outside, as we finally arrive at the train station of the new town. I read the name on the stone building: *Theresienstadt-Bauschowitz*. We walk a long way after the station, to the entrance. Eventually, I see a large sign above the entrance vault.

We are tired and hungry. As we arrive, the reality of the arrangements is a shock. The small apartment we left looks like a palace compared to this place.

We are pointed to a building. We walk over. It is called Dresden Kaserne. My mother, together with my brother, settles in the bunk bed. Is this where the safe place is? Perhaps this is temporary. The vast building smells unclean. Is this Paradise Town?

Dresden Kaserne, our new home.

"*Maminko*, where is father?"

Maminka explains, "Anita, *miláku* (honey), he is going to be in the Ghetto Police, so he will not be living with us."

"Ghetto? What do you mean, there is a ghetto here?"

"Yes, this is a ghetto," she answers, whispering as if these words would get us in trouble.

"But I thought we were going to a safe little town. I don't understand." I reply.

My brother is sitting on his bed clutching his bear Poky in his arms. He looks confused, as if waiting for the train to stop again. As it turns out we never see our bags again. What was I thinking? Valet services... same as what we had in hotels in the Alps? We are not living in the world I have known all my life. We are living in a nightmare. It is beyond any child's dream of monsters in the closet. Why did they deceive us like that? If that were up to me, I would ask for a return ticket.

Eventually, my mother and I exchange an understanding glance. I go over and sit next to Michal. Behind us, in a far bed, I hear someone moan. An old woman is lying in pain. I look at my mother. She looks back. No one speaks.

I settle for this arrangement without any further questions, ignoring the real intent behind it all, accepting the uprooting of our family and now the division of our strong family cell.

Mom says, "Anita, you should be glad we are together. Before the epidemic of encephalitis, they separated children from their parents."

"Do you mean all girls together?" I ask. "That would be kind of fun in a way."

"Anita, you do not know what you are saying. That's why they contracted the virus. That killed a lot of young ones of encephalitis."

"I am sorry Mom. I miss having friends so much, you know. I want to play with other kids my age. What is encephalitis?"

"It is a terrible illness that gives one fever and seizures and kills..."

While my mother is speaking, a young girl comes over and says, "I am Olga, are you new?"

"Yes," I say, a bit suspicious at first.

"I can show you around!"

She wears old clothes. Her dark brown hairs are tightly braided. She looks thin and tall. Her hands are not clean. Red bites are covering hands and face,

"I need to look after my brother," I answer.

There are about two hundred people in our barrack, but I hear we are lucky because we have bunk beds.   In others, people are sleeping on thin mattresses on the floor. Our barrack is one of many. Every one of them has a name.

At dinnertime, a carrier brings food to the entrance of our barrack. It is turnip and potato soup, the mainstay of what we will eat, with the bread. Vegetables are cut up or mashed up. There is no meat or milk. We eat on our beds, crouched on our knees. Plates and cups are made of aluminum, like soldiers or campers.

We all look at each other in disbelief, when plates arrive. Is this a meal? Some venture a nibble, but quickly push their plates away. The broth of the soup is dark and is tasteless. In the next plate, potatoes are watery, and there is no sign of meat. At first, we do not want to eat. Others willingly take our food. It changes quickly as we become too hungry to be choosy.

In the next few weeks, we are in shock, but about we are surviving, trying to adapt to this new living arrangement. I want to make friends and play ball with the boys. We don't see my father too often. However, the Ghetto Police job gives him some advantage to get around.

The Jewish Council for Elders organizes the ghetto. Jakob Edelstein, a fervent Zionist in favor of creating Israel, was nominated first Judenältester (Jewish Elder) of the Jewish Council of Elders in the ghetto.

***

Edelstein and his associates were determined to prevent further deportations to the East. They organize a self-sustaining, productive community, Germans would find indispensable to their war effort.

Jüdische   Arbeit zur Rettung jüdischen Lebens— Jewish work to save Jewish *lives*—was the idea behind Edelstein's policy.

The Austro-Hungarian journalist Theodor Herzl formally established the modern Zionist movement in the late nineteenth century. In response to pogrom, he believed strongly in the formation of a country for Jewish people.

***

I am eager for any small piece of news coming our way. Here we learn a lot. Various people bring information. Some of them used to be teachers. They are sharing about Jewish history and how our past has repeated itself, yet we needed to remain *shtark* (strong).

Mr. Sartinsky tells us about a situation in Paris: How violence on our part might have brought on worse consequences. Here is his story: "A few years ago, a young man named Herschel Grynszpan, born of Polish parents, lived in Hanover, Germany. He faced significant prejudices in school. Therefore, he went to school in a Yeshiva (Jewish School) in Frankfurt. He studied Hebrew and the Torah. He went to Paris to stay with a small Yiddish-speaking enclave of Polish Orthodox Jews. Again, he faced rejection by French officials, so he could not work or study legally. He belonged to a youth organization called Tsukunft.

In response to rising anti-Semitism in the 1930s, Tsukunft organized a militia. This disciplined paramilitary organization, which had a chain of command, organization, and uniforms, played an important role in protecting locals and activities.

During his stay, Herschel (Hermann in German) learned that his parents' resident permits in Germany were canceled. Jewish residents were not going to be able to stay and were expelled from Germany.

In March 1938, Poland had passed a law depriving Polish citizens who had lived continuously abroad for more than five years of their citizenship. In October of the same year, 12,000 Jewish Germans of Polish origin were arrested, stripped of property, and herded aboard trains headed to Poland. The streets were full of people shouting, "Juden raus! Aus nach Palästina!" ("Jews get out! Out to Palestine!") When they got to Poland, Poland refused to admit them.

The postcard Herschel Grynszpan received was from Zbąszyń (Bentschen). The postcard reached him on

November 3. On November 7, he wrote a farewell card to his parents. He presented himself at the German Embassy, 78 Rue de Lille, armed with a revolver he had just purchased recently.

'I am from Germany, and I need to see a German official.'

'Yes, sir, I will see who can speak with you.'

The clerk picked up the telephone and requested an official. The clerk hung up and said, 'Herr Vom Rath will see you.' Mr. Vom Rath was a junior official.

'Thank, you,' said Herschel.

He walked up to the room where the clerk pointed. He entered the room, where Herr Vom Rath greeted him, 'Guten Morgen (Good morning).'

The response from Herschel was not what Vom Rath expected, 'You're a filthy Boche....' He raised his revolver and shot him five times in the abdomen.
He did not attempt to resist or escape the French Police. He confessed to the shooting and explained that it is to avenge the persecuted German Jews.

The postcard to his parent was also found:

With God's help, my dear parents, I could not do otherwise. May God forgive me; the heart bleeds when I hear of your tragedy and that of the 12,000 Jews. I must protest so that the whole world hears my protest, and that I will do. Forgive me. — Hermann"

After Mr. Sartinsky finishes this story, many questions are raised.

"What is your take on what happened?" One of the boys asks.

"So what about Kristallnacht?" Another older boy, who seems knowledgeable about the story, asks.

Mr. Sartinsky answers, "We will talk about this next. Hold your question."

Another question comes, "I am wondering. Can you explain why we are being chosen to be bad guys? We work hard. I think my parents are smart and live consciously. What is it about us?"

Mr. Sartinsky pauses, looks away, and then starts to speak with a very calm voice. Behind his brown beard, the blue eyes are very grave.

"Young people, these are good questions. Perhaps, you can tell me the answers?"

"My father said people often do not like smart people," someone says.

Another boy says, "Yes, and society sometimes needs scapegoats."

Mr. Sartinsky takes over. "Well, it's not too far from the general impression. You are correct. No one likes to have people better than themselves. It's a reality. So what can one do to avoid this situation? Is there an answer?"

"Pray?" a girl ventures.

"Be humble?" Another says.

I finally shared my concerns, "Are we here because of this Hermann Herschel person from Poland? If so, we are not Polish: we are Czech, and I don't see what this story has to do with us!"

The deaths of my grandparents and our latest move have me kind of angry and annoyed. I need to get it out.

Food arrives, and we all disband.

At night, we often go to sing in a choir. We rehearse *Brundibar* (Bumble Bee).

Our director, Hans Krasa, is a very diligent music director. I always feel good after I return to our barrack after practice. The story of this opera is something that gives me hope. Especially in the final song:

"The Victory March: We've won a victory over the tyrant mean.... We've won a victory, since we were not fearful...bright, joyful, and cheerful.... He who loves his mom and dad, mother, and native land, who wants the tyrant's end, join us hand in hand, and be our welcome friend...."

The happy feelings we have after singing do not last. Our singing group is changing constantly. New children are coming. And those who had been rehearsing with us have left. Where did they go?

CHAPTER 17

Living

Spring 1942–Summer 1943

Drawing by Terezín children, 1943.

Most of my time is spent playing ball. I went to visit my mother at work yesterday. The room was dark and filled with clothes and objects. She was emptying suitcases full of clothes.

"*Maminko*, why do you have to empty these travel bags? Can't people who arrive do it for themselves?"

"Anita, *milák* (dear), these are from people who no longer can."

"What do you mean?"

She pauses. I can tell she isn't going to tell me the truth. The way she looks away searching for words...

"Well, you know; like Grandma or Uncle Heintz, they might have decided not to stay with us."

As I am looking at the clothes she handles. I recognize a dress. That dress belonged to one of the girls in the singing group of *Brundibar*.

I know what she tells me does not add up. People are not dying voluntarily. I get it now; for many, it isn't a choice. Are we actually using the clothes of people who have just died under the hand of the Nazis? Now that I have put away all my fantasies of kings and queens I know better.

"Mother. Don't polish the truth. I am twelve now."

I can see the clock in my head. In my eyes, I have reached adulthood.

"*Maminko,* I know. I know what is going on. I know you do not really want to do this, like *tatinek* does not want to work for the ghetto police. Germans force it on us: I understand - no need to veil our lives."

"All right, Anita, you are precious. I don't want to see you grow up too quickly."

Mother is still desperately hoping I won't grow up as fast as life is forcing itself into my innocent mind. I sit next to her. I take an enormous breath trying to sound cheerful and strong. However, my whole body seems to be shaking inside, from hunger or fear.

"I think we need to make the best of this *Maminko.*"

"You are such an optimist, Anita. I suppose you are right in some way. The Jewish Council is trying hard. and everyone is sharing his or her talents and knowledge, like the music director. I think your performance of *Brudibar* is coming along nicely."

"Yes, I love singing. It brings hope. Our music director said the Allies are working on coming to rescue all of us."

Maminka smiles, gives me a hug and a kiss, and sends me off to look after my brother.

Every plane passing over the town is a new hope for me. As I go to sleep on the bunk bed, I am trying to imagine what the world knows now.

When will they come?

Will they be here in time?

News from the outside is not readily available, except by word of mouth. When I was playing soccer with the boys I heard that a boy named Weiner has started a newsletter, he calls it *Rim Rim*.

***

December 1941 holds a special memory: the United States entered the war, and we were hoping to be liberated. Every little piece of news was so important. We were holding on to one day, week and month.

Summer 1942

Hunger. We are forever hungry, counting minutes to the next meal, waking up in the middle of the night. Hunger is slowly encroaching on us emotionally, and still no rescue in sight.

My brother says to my mother, "*Maminko*, I am hungry."

My mother stands there with tears rolling down her cheeks. My brother never asks again.

There is also a secret code of conduct going around in town. We are never to use any German words in our conversation, like we did before. Anyone who does is looked at cross-eyed as a sympathizer of the Germans.

Summer 1943

Today, our family is both sad and jubilant at the same time. My cousins from Praha have arrived and are with us. Even though we did not want them to be sent here, we are all pleased to see them. My mother is hugging her sister. They are both in tears. They have so much to discuss. What is happening in Praha?

I lose interest quickly with all the tears. My cousin Paul is here. From this day forward, he is part of the soccer team too.

The town has now about 40,000 of us. Except for the way we live—dormitory style and eating camp style—and for the constant nagging hunger. I have been very busy with many activities. The Jewish Council has been working on a library.

Ubožátko (poor thing), Michal has been very ill. He has contracted something they call hepatitis. After our last visit to the infirmary, for what they called a test, we all turned different shades of yellow. I did not feel sick, but Michal has been in bed for weeks. My mother keeps repeating, "*mizerný...mizerný* (miserable)." Mother's eyes are sunken, and she rarely smiles. Her tired clothes are so *baňatý* (baggy) on her.

Today, I visit with my father.

"Oh, my *miláčku*," he says.

He looks sad, not the father I remember. He seems preoccupied and despondent.

"What's up, *tatinek*?"

"Anita, if you go home before me, don't forget the piano..." a silence follow, he swallows, "... in storage, you know?"

"Of course, Father, but why do you think you would stay?" All of a sudden I am so worried, remembering what happened with Uncle Heintz.

"Well, you never know, *miláčku*. The camp is pretty full. Just last year, they took two thousand people to Riga, they say. It's all the way up north."

"Oh, *tatinek*, don't think of the worst." A silence follows.

"*Tatinek*, are you still singing for the Requiem with Schächter?"

"Anita, I have not been able to stand too long; I get dizzy. You know our water resources are very limited. Typhoid fever is becoming an issue. I am afraid to drink, and it tastes bad, because of disinfectants," he coughs.

"What is wrong? You are coughing." I say.

"I don't know," he answers.

I reply, "I am afraid of going to the health clinic too. Last time the doctor gave me an injection, he said, it would save a lot of people's lives."

"Oh no, Anita. Your mother did tell me about Michal being sick. That was horrible, I was so worried about your brother."

"I know. I was afraid he was not going to survive. You should have seen how weak he was."

My father continued: "I am helping on a movie the Jewish Council has to prepare. Gerron is the producer. It is for the Red Cross and other countries, so they know good things about this town. The name of the movie is: *The Führer Gives a Village to the Jews.*

"Interesting! What a gift, eh? So many are sick!"

"Anita. You won't believe the movie, it's all made up. It's not our real lives. It's what they want the outside world to believe. It is sickening. I am ashamed to participate."

I take my father's hand.

"Let's go for a walk, like in the old time, Father."

He has changed so much, I barely recognize him. He has lost all his vigor. He seems so betrayed and beyond anger.

I am walking back to our barrack and thinking of what people have told us about the *Untermensch*—a term used by some because of the propaganda. I am trying so hard to be positive with my friends and within myself. I can see how this term is describing what we have become: sub-human. There is no way we will let this plan succeed.

***

When the International Red Cross came to check on our fate, the Nazis were one step ahead of them. They hid the sick and dying, and trotted forth-new arrivals that were still in relatively good health. Our carefully coached inmates cheered each other on the soccer field. The visitors were guests of honor at a charming make-believe soiree featuring our children's opera group.

The Red Cross delegation went off, satisfied. The Germans also shot propaganda footage of the "happy" Theresienstadt inhabitants. But not by the film's stars, who were soon on their way to destiny. Who says pictures don't lie?

This film was about the Czechoslovakian city named Theresienstadt, given to the Jews for preparations to deport them to either Israel or Madagascar.

The GPO. General Plan was a secret Nazi German plan for the colonization of Central and Eastern Europe. Implementing it would have necessitated genocide and Ethnic cleansing to be undertaken on a vast scale in these European territories occupied by Germany during World War II.

A hepatitis epidemic spread across wide areas of Europe, leaving no doubt about the previously questioned infectious nature of the disease. The losses in the German army from hepatitis presented a challenge. German scientists needed to identify the infective agent via animal trials and experiments with humans. Arnold Dohmen carried out experiments on Jewish children.

At the same time my father was s grieved by the loss of his power to care for us, the parting of our belongings as well as the loss of his own parents. I could not appreciate at the time the significance of his preoccupation with our piano. It represented what he had worked so hard to build for his family. His love of music and singing the opera that bonded our love for each other.

CHAPTER 18

The Day

*I*t hangs over our head for weeks. The Jewish Council is working on lists. The town of Terezín has become too populated. With the continual arrival of new people, we are living like the fish in cans. Like those, we used to eat. The news has come that we will be sent elsewhere. Now it is just a question of time. The Jewish Council is preparing lists of persons who have to leave.

My brother and I are active, but together barely tip the scale at 50 kg (110 lbs.). The Maccabi Athletics Club could never have prepared us for years of hunger. We are so hungry. Our minds are controlled by our need to eat. Yet, we never steal from each other. Nevertheless, anything that can lead us to food is a priority.

One day, I decide to volunteer for the gardening crew. I always hope that for all the work and efforts we offer, my family will receive some special consideration. However, it seems in vain. The SS (Schutzstaffel) officers are guarding the garden with rifles. Our clothes do not have any pockets. We are inspected on the way out to make sure we have not garnished our pockets with pounds of lettuce or beets.

Many are sick with typhoid, and another T disease, TB I think. Everyone is very apprehensive and worried. We are eagerly going from place to place in the ghetto trying to get news.

It is almost now two years since we heard of Pearl Harbor. At that time, the Japanese declared war against the United States. I had the false impression then that they were to liberate us anytime soon. Nevertheless, over the past two years many planes have passed over the town but nothing has happened. Still every time a plane comes close, my heart is full of hope and beats hard with expectations. Is it going to be today?

Two years ago, news spread that the United States went to North Africa. Why Africa? We are here in Czechoslovakia, town of Theresienstadt. I feel like screaming at the top of my lungs, "We are here, please, please, come and save us!" Why did Japan attack the US Navy in Pearl Harbor? It is so very complicated.

News is important to us and every time someone reports a fresh fact or event. It spreads like wildfire from person to person.

My brother now is eight. I'll be thirteen this year. It has been almost two years that we have lived in the ghetto of Terezín.

"We are golden, Michal, we are." I say, as I am jumping with enthusiasm.

"What for?" he replies with a gruff tone.

"I heard another plane, I understand they are now over Berlin."

"Really. What took them so long? I wonder," replies Michal.

"I know. We have to try to stay strong and keep fighting. There is no sense in being overtaken with pessimism."

I sense I have to keep a positive spirit for our family. I do have a secret, however—there is a boy. He is a soccer star, a goalie. However, there is a drawback. He is a little older. He is nineteen and also...well...he has a girlfriend. I am envious of her. Aside from that, it keeps me hoping. I still play soccer with the boys. Girls have questions for me about the boys. However, all these romances are interrupted one day.

My father stops by, breathless, and says, "We are it. We are on the list. Be ready at dawn."

"Oh! Fritz." My mother starts, "Where are we going? Do you know?"

Tatinek is very grave. He is untying his heavy shoes, and he looks defeated. Despite all his efforts, he is unable to protect us from further moves. I am not so sure why my father is so upset about the news. What could be worse? He says to mother.

"Stela, I don't know anymore. We have to hope for the best. At least, we will be together. It has been going on for a while. There are just too many of us in the ghetto. I know so many families who have no idea where their children are. We are fortunate to still be close even if under different roofs."

I am feeling very nervous and uneasy about the news. I sense the state of panic my mother is in, and the dark place my father inhabits. Rather than letting myself slide into hysteria; I decide to turn the event into an adventure for my brother.

I sit next to Michal and say, "Michal. Tomorrow is going to be an *eskapáda* (escapade). We are going to be fleeing. Get ready with all your little things in your bag." We no longer have luggage. We turned our bags in when we arrived. Nevertheless, we have accumulated small treasures: a piece of dried bread too hard to eat, pebbles, stones, a walnut, anything worth keeping.

Michal looks at me in disbelief,

"So how come *maminka* and *tatinek* don't talk? If it were so good, our parents would be happy."

"Well, *miláku*, they are planning a route." There is no return from my fantasies. I have to come forth.

"You see; there are tunnels throughout the countryside," I continue, not sure where I am going to go with my tale.

Michal is now lying down, looking at me with his big eyes full of hope. Fueled by the results my fables have on Michal, I continue.

"Well, in these tunnels we will also find food left by the Allies for us."

Hunger has given me a prolific imagination. Like a mirage, I can see these passageways. No matter how dark they are, they are abundant with delicious food. Lovely food like we had before all of this happened, in our dining room, the one with the green furniture—ham and colorful vegetables, deserts, cake with frosting and my piano. So my story goes on, and when I look down, Michal is asleep.

To tell you the truth, I hope that tomorrow he does not remember what I just said. Could my story give him just a good night of innocent sleep? The fleas are biting more than ever. I lie down next to him and cover him with our shared blanket. I wonder what has gotten into me, to come up with such a fable. Is it my wishes, perhaps something to hold on to? No one else heard it. It is our secret again.

Morning comes like a light. My mother is calling, "Anita, Michal, up. Get ready."

***

Of course, I had no idea the rest of the world was in turmoil. I had no idea of the thousands who were in a similar place like us all over Europe. The master plan of the madman was probably still unclear to most.

The actions of the United States after Pearl Harbor and their entry into the war were not as direct as we had hoped—first the Pacific, then North Africa. Efforts by the Allies were well orchestrated. Nonetheless, there were successes, and there were defeats. The U.S. had wished to remain neutral before Pearl Harbor.

The outcome of World War I left them hesitant. Therefore, Roosevelt had offered assistance through the Lend-Lease Act, signed on March 11, 1941.

The gymnastic club we belonged to before 1939, the Maccabi Club, was founded in late nineteen hundred by Zionist believers. The mission was to encourage Jewish pride and physical fitness.

Maccabi Club, 1935

The Maccabi Club was founded in late nineteen hundred by
Zionist   believers, to encourage Jewish pride and physical
fitness.

CHAPTER 19

Shield of Armor

Drawing by Terezín artist (1941–1944)

My Shield of Armor comes after we leave the town of Terezín.

*I*t is late in the year 1943; it is still dark when we walk to the train station on that morning. It is the same station where we arrived a year and a half ago. We certainly feel different, emaciated and covered with bites from bed bugs and fleas.

This time the trip on the train lasts days. We are packed in cattle cars. There is a bucket in the corner. Sixty people use it to relieve themselves. After a day, the smell is horrible. It is starting to overflow. The smell of ammonia and fecal odor is with us constantly. There is no food or water for the length of the trip. It seems to last forever.

When we finally arrive, I see the name "Auschwitz-Birkenau" inscribed on the gate. There is also an archway that says: "Arbeit Macht Frei." *Work liberates you.*

We are asked to put our bags on the ground and take three steps forward. A few minutes later when we look back, our bags have disappeared. I look at my mother with a silent question written on my face. I think; perhaps they are so kind to bring them to the place where we will stay? I see people behind barbed wires, skinny and sickly looking.

"They look like prisoners, *maminko*?"

"They are," she replies.

"Are we going to be like them?"

"I don't know, but it is very possible."

As she finishes the sentence an officer begins pushing us around, "*SCHNELL, SCHNELL*!" Using a wood stick, he pushes Michal along. It appears as if we are a herd of animals. It is drizzling and cold. Women are screaming ahead of us. Babies are crying. As we go further, babies are torn from their mother's arms. My mother is shaking like leaves during a terrible storm. She is scared that they will take us too. She squeezes my hand so tightly that a small gouge is left in my palm. When I open my hand, I see blood.

The night is coming. We are frightened and tired. Officers are screaming, "*AUSZIEHEN, AUSZIEHEN* (Undress)." The large-necked woman officer screams as if we are stone-deaf. We are ordered to enter the first room where we are to remove all our clothes. Those disappear away and next a spray to kill lice and bedbugs. The tone of all these people in uniform is so harsh and rude. I felt brutalized and shaken to tears.

My strength is disappearing. It is humiliating to stand naked in this way. I never experienced any thing similar, even in the previous year in Terezín. I feel angry, and determined not to let this get to me. I build this shield in my head, in order not to appear scared, but defiant and proud.

Next we enter a room with communal showers. The water feels good, but it's cold. I am glad to get rid of insects, which bit us and caused much aggravation for a long time.

As we leave the shower, we are pushed to another room. We leave that area with our head shave or hair, cut very short. The next room holds uniforms and clothes. Sizes are given at random, and we need to figure out how to exchange among each other. Shoes are wooden clogs, like people wear in Holland. We receive a yellow star, communists a red triangle; homosexuals a pink triangle, and gypsies a purple triangle.

The formal camp uniform in Auschwitz is a gray-and-blue-striped denim. Distinguishable at a distance, we learn this uniform makes it difficult to hide in case of escape.

The next room, I am given a new name. It is a number.

"*JETZT gilt es AUF zu passen* (Now, it is vital to pay attention). *Ihr seid jetzt* (you are now):"

I wait for my new name in disbelief.

"EINUNDSIEBZIGTAUSENDFUNFHUNDERT und NEUNUNDSECHZIG. (71569)"

How am I going to remember such a long name? Now we lost our names too.

I am trying to remember the number in my head by repeating it. Fortunately, my mother knows German. We used to speak it at home, but most others from various countries never spoke German and could not repeat their numbers. It is a long number even for me to remember. The officer also explains from this day forward; we need to answer to that number or we will be punished or shot. I help others write down their numbers so they will remember.

Next, the number is tattooed on our arms. Later, we are sent to BIIb (section of Birkenau) camp. It is a camp for people coming from the Theresienstadt Family Camp (Terezín).

I am tired. The little girl inside of me wants to cry, but I hold tears back. I am famished too. I convince myself that a solid armor is best. I do not want anyone to get the satisfaction of seeing me cry. So many hopes, and yet things are worse every time we move. So distant are my dreams of escape tunnels and food.

My thoughts keep going back to the event of Pearl Harbor and our hopes for liberation, but now two years later we are official prisoners. We are hungry, so hungry. The lack of food takes away all our mental power to fight. Having another piece of bread is so much more important. Even so, no one takes anything from one another.

We live now in an army barrack. The conditions are far worse than in our last domicile. A horrible smell lingers everywhere. People are ill. Old people are dying, near death, or already gone. Will this nightmare ever end?

I shiver and feel as if a fever is beginning to invade. I am afraid to talk about it or mention any illnesses. Last time, we received a vaccine for scarlet fever. Doctors were looking for the proper dosage for the vaccine. Fortunately, I was not ill, but my brother was sick for days and worried my mother to death. No one wants to go to the medical wing because those who go get sicker and often do not return.

My brother does not look well. His deep hazel eyes look hazy at times, as if he is fading from us. He rarely talks anymore. I sit next to him and try to bring him back into our world of stories, "Michal, soon we are going to leave this place. The Allies know we are waiting."

As empty-bellied as I am, it is more important to see Michal come back to me. He looks at me, but no words come out of his dried, pale lips.

"Michal, *miláku,* please, eat, please." His eyes seem to hold the deepest secret; he finally says a few words.

"Anita, I don't believe you anymore," he closes his eyes again and shuts his secret inside once more.

160

"What is it?" Tears are rolling down his hollow cheeks.

"You told me we were escaping in a tunnel, Anita." His tears come faster now.

"Oh, Michal. I thought you knew by now. It was just a wish and a dream to help you get through another night. We don't have much control. I just pretended."

"Liar, Anita!" His anger revives his eyes in some mysterious way. He raises his hand with the only strength left in him and punched me lightly. "I thought you did, Anita. Why is it, no one has any control? Just these people dressed in gray uniforms?" Tears continued to drip down his cheeks, now in a deep sob. He hides his face in his hands.

My heart is sinking deeper into my now frail body. I wish I could make this a better place for him, but it is beyond words. At that moment, I feel so much love from my brother; but helpless to give him hope. I take his head onto my lap and stroke his hair without a sound, hoping, the elixir of my touch would do more.

"*Maminko*, do you think we are going to see *tatinek* again?"

"I don't know, Anita," she answers. Her face is pale and gray. Her eyes have lost their glimmer. She looks tired, not the *maminka* I once knew. The uncertainty of this new move is hurting her deeply.

"*Maminko*, what is going to happen?"

The area where we stay is full of forgotten debris. We all slumber on one mattress, afraid to be separated during our sleep, constantly awakened by moaning and crying.

"I don't know, *miláku*." Her eyes are red, and I reflect on my doubts.

"Sorry." Why am I asking such a stupid question? Food is far worse than in Terezín. Sometimes our rations do not come at all. Are we waiting to die? What is this sign? "Arbeit Macht Frei." How can work liberate us if we are just in waiting?

***

Needless to say, the coming year did not bring us a lot of smiles. However, a turn of events soon will bring my own salvation.

CHAPTER 20

Salvation

The paintings of The Holocaust Through Czech Children's Eyes

*O*ne day we hear an announcement. It is first for men than for women.

 "Achtung (attention)! Anyone, eighteen to fifty, who can work must sign up to go to Germany to work."

I am thirteen going on fourteen. My mother looks at me.

"Anita. Go sign up. Tell them you are eighteen."

"Mom, they'll never believe me."

""You never know," she answers.

I turn to her with pleading eyes, remembering the experience in the garden with armed officers.

"Will you come too?"

She answers with tears rolling down her cheeks, "I can't, Anita. If I leave your brother, he will forget his name, and we will never find him."

I take a few steps and consider her suggestion. Does she not love me, to let me go to work? After further reflection, I decide that whether my mother loves me is not the issue. I don't mind working. Perhaps, I'll get closer to my father who is out working somewhere. Since we arrived, we only saw him once, from a distance. He was signing out to go to work. He is with other men in a different camp and can't leave.

Again, I remember my job of volunteering in the gardens at the ghetto. I liked working, even though it was under gunpoint. I am not looking forward to a similar experience, but perhaps this will bring something better. One never knows.

When the officer asks my date of birth, I tell her June 1, 1926. The officer looks at me intensely. These are the longest seconds. She finally says, "Richtig, bist du soweit? (Good, are you ready?" Then she motions for me to join the line. All the women march to Auschwitz. I leave feeling abandoned by *maminka,* and I cry all the way from Birkenau to Auschwitz.

Here we undergo a selection. We undress and line up in front of Dr. Mengele. I am with older women. My stomach is torn in fear. It suddenly feels as if my insides are going to open and empty at once. I run to the latrine. I know something is wrong. It will be my end if I stay in this line. Once there, I realize I can't go back out. It is a moment of insanity or perhaps clarity.

Since I am small, I make my way to a different line with younger women. Now as my turn comes up to go in front of the doctor under his piercing black eyes, I turn at an angle, allowing me to hide my chest

He has not noticed I am underage. I make it to the accepted line. I feel so terrified during this time that I forget how starved I feel. All the other girls are tall and well formed.

Now we go to the women's section where only SS women are doing examinations. For a moment, I lose control of the emotions I had guarded so preciously. I start to cry uncontrollably.

"I am only thirteen. I want to go back to my mother...I am only thirteen...." I am crying so hysterically that one of the examiners takes me to the side into a separate room. She gives me cocoa. For an instant, I see for the first time, warmth in the eyes of an officer.

***

Throughout my experience in the camps, I see glimpses of humanity in the SS officers. This moment is one of my most memorable experiences. This woman saves my life.

***

She says, "How come you speak German?"

"My mother is from the borders where they speak German."

166

"Really?" she says again with some warmth in her round face.

"Yes, and my mother went to school in Vienna."

"You know, I understand how you miss your mother, but know that you are better off going to the work camp.

"Why is that?"

"I can't explain, but I know. Please don't go back," she taps me on the shoulder kindly. Her touch feels warm and trustworthy.

My tears slowly dry, and I resign myself to her suggestion. I join the transport of 500 women. On the same day, we embark for our new destination. This trip is the worst ever. Leaving my family tears me apart, yet I still feel angry at my mother. I feel lost in a sea of other people I do not know. No shoulder to lean against. The smell of urine does not reach me, for the inner torment is far worse.

It is dark outside when we leave. The night feels bottomless. The faint chatter of other girls seems endless. My heart still aches despite the armor I regained, thanks to the woman officer. I slowly retreat into a fetal position. I have seen dogs sleep this way. Perhaps, it will help.

***

There are no words to express the suffering and humiliation I felt during these years. The progressive degradation we are undergoing, the tearing apart of our family strength, the fears, the continuous hunger, feelings of destitution, and unfairness of it all. There is no word that can adequately describe it. I think only people who have suffered similar fates can truly understand. Yet, so many things happen along the way to keep me alive and hoping.

***

When I wake up, it is light again. There is a girl next to me. She has a very maternal look in her eyes. She says, "Did you sleep well? You seemed so tired. You did not move at all for hours."

It feels somehow like the beginning of a new life. I sit up and look at her.

"Yes, I did. Who are you?"

"My name is Ruth. I come from Prague. I was in college when we were told to leave. Here I am, with no idea where the rest of my family is."

Map of work camps in and around Hamburg.

Marion A. Stahl

CHAPTER 21

Arbeit Macht Frei

*I*t takes me weeks to get used to leaving my mother behind. I have never been separated from my family before. I am still mad at my mother for sending me away to a work camp. Now I am with 500 other women and the youngest of all of them. We are sent to work in the trenches and at the harbor to unload boats.

Fortunately, Ruth and other older college girls have adopted me as their youngest sister and I start feeling more at ease. We sleep in very large storage buildings in a shipyard. At night, we hear the small steps of creatures coming from the water. We figured out a way to sleep completely covered up with our thin mattress, so we aren't found in their inquisitive searches.

It feels as if our lives are reduced to those of animals: Sleeping on dirty floors, hiding from vermin at night. However, I want to live. I want to eat. Food has been more available now with work. Tonight, Ruth is sleeping next to me under the mattress. The blanket on the floor is prickly, but feels warmer than the cement.

"Ruth, where do you think your parents are?" I ask.

"I don't know Anita, but I think of them every night before I go to sleep, my younger sister Anna too. I certainly hope they didn't take them and that they escaped to a safe country. Perhaps, they went to Palestine. I know my father had a plan, but because I was in college they had no control when we were sent away."

"I get it. What a wretched war. How could one not stop a yobo like Hitler? Is this unbelievable?"

"A yobo? What a good name, Anita. He is that, alright."

"Ruth, I know. I like to invent and sometimes dream of things, which don't exist. One day when we were leaving the ghetto to go to Auschwitz, I made up this story of escaping—"

I hear Ruth's regular even breaths. I think she is asleep. I think of how angry Michal was at me for making up the story.

The air raids are regular now on Hamburg. Usually, they are aimed at oil refineries, and we run into the woods when the bombing starts.

At some point, the forest nearby is bombed. A shell hit very close, and we are covered in dirt. A soldier is running. He trips over my dirt-covered leg and falls. He apologizes. He is one of our guards. I still feel confused by what has just happened. I say:

"Thank you. I am not sure what really just happened."

He replies:

"I know you. You are the girl who works so hard. You are digging trenches better than most. What is your name?"

I am a bit afraid. It is the man in the olive uniform and spotless boots that patrols our work.

"A...A...Anita," I stutter. "Anita Pollakova."

We waited to see if further raids were coming.

He asks, "How old are you?"

I first got up and shook the dirt off, "August 11. I'll be fourt...I am eighteen."

Finally, I decide to tell the truth.

"I tell every one that I'm eighteen, but I'm really fourteen." I expect him to get angry, but the man closes his eyes for a second, looking as if he is shocked and needing to process what I just said.

"You're fourteen? Fourteen?!"

The soldier is sort of old, like my father. His eyebrows are getting closer, and creases appear.

"My goodness... the world really has ended. Children are brought in the midst this disaster."

Finally, he reaches for his backpack. I am shaking uncontrollably. I expect him to take out a gun and shoot me. He must have now realized that I am underage for the job. I take a step back, ready to run.

"No, no. Come here," he says gently.

Reluctantly, I take a few steps forward.

Out of his backpack, the Wehrmacht soldier draws a paper sack. Slowly, I watch him remove one layer then the next. It is a sandwich. I stop shaking and smile. I can't remember the last time I saw a real sandwich outside of my imagination.

"This is for you," he says, breaking the sandwich in half.

"Oh, no sir," but my eyes reveal clearly my true feelings.

I take what he gives me in disbelief. I stare at it, to make sure it is real.

"Thank you," I reply and turn to walk away.

"Wait, do not leave. You are hungry. I don't want you to share that with the others. I want you, and only you, to eat it; all of it."

That act of kindness touches me. Good things happen, and that moment gives me new hope.

From then on, every day the man gives me half of his sandwich. We sit and eat together. I learn during that time that he had been once a professor and taught French at a local university. I tell him about my family, that my brother and parents are at work sites in different towns and that I am here alone.

At some point, he asks.

"When is your birthday?"

"In August," I reply.

"That's soon. What would you like?"

I have not thought of what I want in a while, let alone for my birthday. What do I want? Toys? No. A horse? No. I look out toward the ocean. Yes, I know what I want.

"I want to go swimming in the ocean."

"That's all?" He looks confused.

"Yes, in Czechoslovakia, where I use to live, there are only lakes, no oceans. I remember my mother taking me for swimming lessons with my little brother, Michal, after we went to the tennis club. I always looked forward to those swimming lessons. I love swimming and the sea looks incredible."

"All right, I will give you my whole sandwich; you don't have to work, and you can swim in the ocean. You have to promise that you won't run away."

"I promise."

Several weeks have passed. We are still cleaning up after each attack. What we find in the ruins is intense; legs, arms, objects, babies—seldom alive. Sometimes we find food or a treasure; however, soldiers are quick to confiscate them.

As my birthday approaches, I realize that I am very excited. All I can think about is what it will feel like to breaststroke and freestyle in the blue waters of the ocean. Then, here it is. August 11 has arrived and the Wehrmacht soldier is present.

"Happy Birthday, Anita."

He hands over his full sandwich.

"You deserve it. You work so hard."

I want to hug him, but know that could be compromising.

"Thank you, officer."

I eat the sandwich.

"So are you ready for your real present?" I nod, unable to contain my excitement. We walk down to the sea shore.

"All right Anita, here it is. But before you go, you must promise me again that you will not swim away."

"I promise," I say, and then I dive in the water.

The water rushes over my body. It absorbs me into its powerful arms of cold ripples. I swim, and swim, and swim. Now the soldier looks like an olive dot on the shore. In the distance, ahead, I see a shore lined with beautiful houses.

Houses, yes. I think of our old home in Czechoslovakia: our apartment, my father's piano, my grandmother's cooking, and my mother's smile. Then I think about the shore behind me: the digging, the hard work, and the hunger. How inviting those houses looked. I know that I am close enough; I could easily swim there. I glance back. I can still see the olive-green speck in the distance, the soldier. I think of the lunches together, the way he watches out for me while I work, his life as a professor. I remember my promise not to swim away. I glance at the colorful houses one last time and turn around to start swimming back. I swim slowly, holding each stroke, as long as I can. When I finally arrive back at the shore, the soldier is still waiting in the same spot where I left him.

"How was it?" he asks.

I scan the horizon for the row of houses. I spot them now, a tiny row of black dots. I look back at the soldier, "Unbelievable," I whisper out of breath, "Absolutely incredible."

The birthday is over. It is time to return to the old routine. However, that special day stays with me. We spend the day with our assigned jobs like loading boats with bricks. I like the brick passing - two at a time and two more. I like mixing cement and pushing wheelbarrows. For me, it is all a game that brings food.

We are in Hamburg. It is about 550 miles from where I left my parents and brother. I miss them terribly, but days go by quickly. This work camp is a new survival challenge for me. I take each assignment seriously. I do not mind working hard.

Sometimes I wish that perhaps someone, like that soldier will notice how much I am working and give me a break. At the end of the day, we are exhausted. Well, at least we actually get food. They must realize that if we are not fed, we cannot work.

Ruth and I usually eat next to each other. We eat on our knees the soup we are given today. It is potatoes and more potatoes.

"Anita, I think we are getting a deal today. I believe there are two types of potatoes in this soup." Ruth says.

"How do you know?" I reply.

"Maybe, it's turnip?" Ruth continues.

"Turnip? I never liked them. Well, perhaps, my taste changed."

"Yes, I know for sure. I am eating to survive. However, when I think of my grandmother's pies or my mothers stew, I could give everything for one of those."

"Yes, I know what you mean."

First, it is summer, but then it becomes progressively colder. During the worst cold month, we develop frostbite. Some of us just fall asleep while at work. They call this hypothermia, so we try to keep them awake so they don't die.
Our cotton clothes don't keep us warm, just the coat. However, some are short and cannot fully cover us. There are also other groups of people like us, working. They are

political prisoners from Russia. At this time, I now realize that Jewish people are not the only ones in camps. A man has come closer to us.

"What do you want?" says one of the women from our group.

He is not able to speak our language, and what he says is hard to understand. He has a loaf of bread under his coat and points to it.

The woman comes closer. She takes the bread.

"Thank you," she says. She hides it under her clothes. We share it later.

She is a good woman. She told us one day, "I lost my two children; they were taken away or sent elsewhere...."

Her face is round, and her cheeks hollow. Her eyes are blue. She speaks Czech with a German accent like my mother. Her eyes fill with tears as she talks about her lost children. Her feelings are catching. I long for my mother's arms and the sweet smell of *maminka*. I tell her my story to console her.

"My girl was twelve when we left Praha, my boy ten. They became ill with high fevers. Someone says it was encephalitis. They were in separate quarters with others."

Another woman says, "So is it why they did not separate us perhaps?"

My heart sinks as I listen to this story and realize it could be me. It could be my mother. I am comforted to be alive. Our short break is over; we get back to work.

Initially, we worked for the brick factory, and then when Allies came closer, we dig trenches. Now, Hamburg is bombed often and we clean up the mess afterward. My feet are covered with blisters and I put paper to keep them from oozing. Showers are a rarity. The smells of our unwashed clothes and bodies have become the norm. As long as food comes our way, it's all we really want.

It is a cold day in January now. Everything looks gray and misty. There is no snow, but a wind reaching down to the insides of our bones. Trees look as if they will never grow leaves again. Someone has started a fire to keep the group warm during a break. We lean over close to the source of the warmth, sitting in a circle. Suddenly, a woman starts to shake; slowly, it progresses to her whole body.

"Oh, *Mein Gott*, I think this is a seizure," says one of the older ladies. She gets up and calls for help.

"Can someone come and help?" She calls. But no one responds from among the officers, they are as frozen as we are.

We are so cold and tired we barely move ourselves. Alice, the woman who just had the seizure is spread on the ground, motionless now.

"I think she is not breathing," says the older woman.

I shiver. Ruth holds my hand quietly.

We are so cold and tired we barely move ourselves. Alice, the woman who just had the seizure is spread on the ground, motionless now.

"It is time to get back to work," an officer calls. The sick woman is taken away.

A red mark is painted on the back of our coats. That is how people know who we are and what we are doing. When we go from one place to another, we need to march in rows of five. We are under gun surveillance as we work.

When incoming prisoners arrive, they are assigned a camp ID that is sewn to their prison uniforms. Later, I realize that only those prisoners selected for work are issued IDs. Prisoners sent directly to the gas chambers are not registered and received no tattoos.

At times, I stop and ponder. It has been more than two and half years now that the Allies have been looking for us. Here, instead, we are cleaning up the mess they caused rather than being liberated. This does not make sense.

We have been recruited to fix the mess, but through the time in Hamburg, bombing continues. Every night we go to sleep, we never know if we will see another day. Each day, I work hard to get food. I fall into a deep sleep afterward and dismiss any bombing attacks.

I have lost all trust in the Allies and faith that we will see the end of the war. Fortunately, thanks to all the girls and Ruth, I feel surrounded by good company. Any time we find an opportunity to get away, we do.

There is a tree full of red mouth-watering apples. We can't resist and decide to climb on it and pick them. Eventually, an officer finds out and many of the young women are beaten for it. I tell the officer:

"How could you prevent us from eating? We are hungry. We need to eat to work."

Surprisingly, he does not beat me as he did the others.

In February of that winter (1945), we are told that the Allies are near, and we are relocated to a new camp. Are they trying to hide us?

***

The Battle of Hamburg, code named Operation Gomorrah, was a campaign of air raids beginning July 24, 1943, for eight days and seven nights. At the time, it was the heaviest assault in the history of aerial warfare and was later called the Hiroshima of Germany by British officials.

Until the focus of RAF (Royal Air Force) bomber switched to Hamburg, it had been on the Ruhr industrial region, which had been the target of a five-month long campaign.

By now, merely fourteen years old, I have witnessed all the human degradation one can imagine: people in all stages of dying, children torn from mothers' arms, people sitting on buckets to relieve themselves. Conditions fit at most for animals in a barn. However, from time to time, I encountered a glimpse of hope. Frequently, I ask myself, how could anyone's self-esteem ever be revived after such treatment? Those times were difficult, but the camaraderie existing between us is what helped us survive.

The use of forced labor in Nazi Germany and throughout German-occupied Europe during World War II took place on an unprecedented scale.

It was a vital part of the German economic exploitation of conquered territories. It also contributed to the mass extermination of populations in German-occupied Europe.

The Nazi Germans abducted approximately twelve million people from almost twenty European countries, about two-thirds of whom came from Eastern Europe. Many workers died as a result of their living conditions, mistreatment and malnutrition, or became civilian casualties of war. At its peak, the forced laborers comprised 20 percent of the German work force. Counting deaths and turnover, about fifteen million men and women were forced laborers at one point, or another during the war.

It is important to remember that while the percentage of Jewish prisoners was about half of those affected, the total loss during this war was enormous. Some of the most striking fatalities were in Poland.

While there is no argument that Hitler abhorred the Jews and caused almost six million to be ruthlessly killed, often non-Jewish victims are tragically forgotten from Holocaust remembrances. Eleven million precious human lives were lost during the Holocaust. Five million of these were non-Jewish. Three million were Polish Christians and Catholics. It would be very sad to forget even one precious life extinguished so ruthlessly. It would be a tragedy to forget five million.

What I also did not know was that Wehrmacht soldiers were drafted soldiers, but SS were all volunteers.

Marion A. Stahl

Marion A. Stahl

CHAPTER 22

The Last Stay

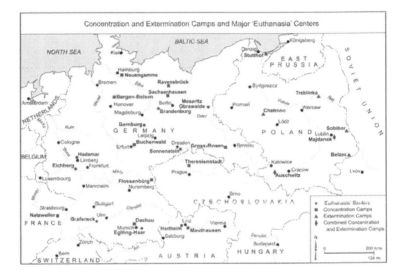

Cartography by Mapping Solutions, Alaska. Source: "Concentration and Extermination Camps and Major 'Euthanasia' Centers," in Jeremy Noakes, ed., Nazism, 1919-1945, Vol. 3: Foreign Policy, War, and Racial Extermination. Exeter: University of Exeter Press, 1998, p. 645.

*F*ebruary 1945. We are going to another camp. Today we arrive in Bergen-Belsen, north of Berlin. When we arrive, I am shocked by what we see. It is by far the worst camp, with many sick and famished people. In some areas, there are piles of unburied dead corpses. The smell is unbearable. I am so frightened this will be me one day. There seem to be more deceased bodies than alive, and if they are still breathing, they are close to death. The sight of this camp is awfully depressing. Is this real? Am I awake, or asleep living a nightmare? No, this is real.

The idea that my mother and brother could be in this state haunts me day and night. Smoke is coming from a building not far away. What are they doing there? It can't be cooking or heating; food is rare and we are hungry, and freezing.

Work camp seems like a good life now. I try to think of happy songs in my head. Fortunately, my friend Ruth and the women are still together. I think of my mother and my dear little brother every day. I can't wait to see them again. I pray my father has figured out a way to escape with them.

Every language is spoken among the inmates: Polish, Russian, French, Czech, Dutch, Lithuanian, Greek. There is no sense of why all these people are here. It is crowded and chaotic. Did I see chimneys smoking like this in Auschwitz?

There are all stages of life. Some are standing and waiting, others are unable to get up, stuck in barracks because they are ill and too weak to walk. They look like skeletons, their skin stretched on their bones, no muscles left to walk. Their ribs and hipbones are showing. Their eyes are gone, as if they can't see us, or perhaps they are dead inside already.

Space is extremely limited. One is lucky if they can find a bunk bed. The camp is overflowing with prisoners. Every day more people are brought into this camp. Food is getting very rare. When will it end? The waiting. A month here seems like an ever-lasting year.

***

While Bergen-Belsen contained no gas chambers, more than 35,000 people died of starvation, overwork, disease, brutality, and sadistic medical experiments.
Bergen-Belsen was a concentration camp near Hanover, in northwest Germany, located between the villages of Bergen and Belsen. Built in 1940, it was a prisoner-of-war camp for French and Belgian prisoners. In 1941, it was renamed Stalag 311 and housed about 20,000 Russian prisoners. By April 1945, more than 60,000 prisoners were incarcerated in Belsen in two camps located 1.5 miles apart. Camp No. 2 was opened only a few weeks before the liberation on the site of a military hospital and barracks.

CHAPTER 23

Konec války

What's next?

*T*oday is the first time I noticed birds outside, again. It is April. The bombing has stopped. Silence is hanging over us. Suddenly, out of nowhere, someone screams, "It's the end of the war. We are free." The echo of everyone who has enough strength to repeat the words follows it:

"It's the end of the war. We are free."

"To koniec wojny. Jesteśmy wolni." (Polish)

"Konec války." (Czech)

"C'est la fin de la guerre. Nous sommes libres." (French)

"Это конец войны. Мы свободны." (Russian)

"Het is het einde van de oorlog. Wij zijn vrij," a Dutch man says.

"It's the end of the war. We are free."

It is mid-afternoon on a Sunday. We notice a tank coming through the gate of Bergen-Belsen, and then we hear: "We are the British Armed Forces and we are here to liberate you."

Many of us run toward soldiers and kiss their hands, and then we hug and kiss each other. It has been years of waiting.

Anyone able to walk is out there, taking the moment into their lungs, into their eyes, a look of disbelief glazing their faces. People are crying, laughing, screaming.

Soldiers enter with the smile of liberators. They quickly change to looks of horror. However, to us, it is the beginning of real salvation and a new life. All I can think of now is finding my family.

***

As the first major camp to be liberated by the Allies, the event received a lot of press coverage. Finally, the world saw the horrors of our lives. Sixty thousand prisoners were present at the time of liberation. Despite the rescue efforts, many survivors continued to die in the camp after the liberation. Five hundred people died daily of starvation and typhus, reaching nearly fourteen thousand. Mass graves were made to hold the thousands of corpses of those who perished.

Mussolini died on April 25, and Hitler killed himself two days later April 30.

After the British army had come into the camp, the doors were open to the world to see what our living conditions were.

The process of liberation took a long time. Evacuation of the camp began on April 21. After being deloused, inmates were transferred to Camp No. 2, where there is an improvised hospital and rehabilitation camp. Barracks were cleared and burned down to combat the spread of typhus.

Between April 18 and April 28, the dead were buried. The SS guards were compelled to collect and bury the bodies.

On May 19, evacuations were completed. The ceremonial burning of the last barracks brought to an end the first stage of the relief operations. In July, the Red Cross took six thousand survivors to Sweden for convalescence, while the rest remained in the newly established displaced persons (DP) camp to await repatriation or emigration.

***

My first view of real life again is at Hanover hospital. I spend an extended quarantine before being released. We are in large wards, and the nurses are so kind to us. Ruth is still with me. We are both waiting for news of our families. Searches for my family have begun. I hear that my father is alive and will be waiting for me in Prague.

I am extremely excited to know he is living. The Red Cross helps me get transportation to my country's capital. I leave in an army truck. On the road to Prague, cherry trees are in bloom. The smell is inebriating.

We finally arrive in the city. The clothes I wear are for survivors. Now I am a grown woman of almost fifteen. We are dropped off at JCC (Jewish Council Center). People were hugging their loved ones, and in tears. I am looking for my father. Tramways and buses are everywhere. I have never been by myself in the capital. There are some volunteers, but not enough to help everyone. One of them has a dark felt hat. She wears a smile on her face, and a pair of glasses with gold rims. She is kind.

My heart is beating fast in expectation of seeing my father again. I have been looking for him every time I see a six-foot man anywhere.

A tall man asks:

"Are you Anita Pollakova, by any chance?"

He is gaunt, my father's age. There is such a good feeling about having my name called again.

"Yes, sir."

He shakes my hand. His face is really sad.

"My name is Karl. Your father sent me here. I see a bench over close to this park. Let's sit down."

I follow him trustingly. As soon as we are sitting, he looks at me with a fatherly face.

"Anita, I am sure you came a long way today to meet your father."

"Indeed sir, I can't wait to see him."

Joy must be written all over my face at the idea of being reunited with my father. The man is silent for a long time.

"What is it, sir? Someone told me needed to come to meet him here."

"Anita, several weeks have passed since you were called to meet your father," he continues.

I look at him with surprise.

"Do you mean to say he is held back from coming today? No problem, it is too bad, but I waited that long. Well, yes, I can understand. I am sure I'll figure a way.... So, where and when will I see him?"

"Anita." He swallows heavily. "I have good news and bad news..."

"Oh?" I do not like the tone of his voice. I become fidgety and anxious. My hands are perspiring in anticipation.

A couple stops by and asks him a question. I look away. I wonder what he means. The bad news and good news...is it about another member of the family? Perhaps he has found my mother, my brother and can't meet me.

The sound of a siren screams in the distance followed by fire trucks.

He starts to speak again:

"The sad news is..." He looks away, pauses and continues:

"... he can't be here. During the death march..." I see his Adam's apple going up and down. I stare at his green eyes, looking for what he is unable to say. He continues:

"'... he was killed. The good news, Anita, is that he died as a hero."

I look at him in disbelief. Who is this man? How could he say that my father died? My father could never die. He is too strong. It's ridiculous.

The man sees that I am struggling with the information he just shared. In the distance, I hear someone crying hysterically. I want to run so as not to hear any more bad news and return just for the good...his words keep repeating in my mind: 'Bad news, good news...'

He finally repeats, "Anita, he died. Germans evacuated his camp. Survivors were forced to walk," he stops, tears are filling his eyes. "During this march he was shot to death."

Images of my emaciated mother and sick brother come to haunt me. Where are they? Did they survive? *Maminka*, Michal... will I find them back home? The piano, the green furniture, our dining room, will they all be there for us again?

Will our family be reunited soon? I see us, healing together in the mountain of snow in front of a fireplace fill my heart and mind—yellowed pictures from the time before all this happened. Memories of my first day on skis, smells of roasted chestnuts, wool blankets, the sled I used to pull my brother. Aunt Hilda, my friend Ilse, our colorful rag puppets and above all, my piano, could these all return? I sit in complete disbelief.

"My father died? But you said he was alive before."

"Yes, I know, Anita. Things changed," he pauses. "They can change so quickly." He looks in the distance as if lost in time.

"But..." I remain in a state of incredulity.

I do not recall clearly the rest of the day. I believe we walked back and sometime later that day, a lady with a dark felt hat and gold-rimmed glasses brought me to an orphanage where I stay until my family is found.

Marion A. Stahl

Despite the announcement, I am refusing to accept it. I continue to look for my father and will for years to come.

Will I find my mother and my brother now?

The kind lady volunteer with the woolen felt hat is accompanying me. Despite the news, I am in complete denial and full of hope for the future and want to close the door to the long nightmare of the war. People are celebrating as we pass the main square and the tower. Smells of roasted meat, flowers box at windows, people singing are promises of renewed future happiness.

EPILOGUE

In this first book, I did not share the feelings a child is inept at formulating. In the next book, I will describe the trials and tribulations I faced in surmounting the emotional damages of the war. How I arrived to who I am today.

I hope it will give faith to those who have suffered similar trauma, as well as veterans of wars. The silver linings of my experiences were numerous: being involved in building Israel as a soldier and a member of a new path, learning to live on a farm in Israel, the experience of working in the field and seeing how we were able to heal and rebuild ourselves, learning to trust again, finding a safe spot in our hearts. It was an incredible journey that I wish to communicate to those who have walked in the same paths. Perhaps others may want to know or learn something from it too.

One of the primary lessons I took from my painful experience is that bullying in its most extreme forms leads eventually to wars and genocide. It not only kills, but also leaves profound scars in those who survive. Ultimately, these scars can render them stronger. Some may become hardened and insensitive and will want retaliation and more war, but hopefully others will advocate peace, as I am.

I will never find any relatives. Despite the devastation and the loss, I manage to survive and will encounter many more positive adventures in my journey. After living in a home for orphans, I was recruited to join the Zionist underground Haganah army and go to Palestine. I lived in a kibbutz with my first husband. Our final home was in the United States, where I raised our son and will see my grandchildren born.

I kept these stories buried for the better part of my life. As I saw my grandchildren growing up, I began to realize I needed to tell my part. It started after my visit to the Holocaust Museum. I went with my Brooklyn-born, second husband and two of my very best friends, the first month it opened, twenty years ago.

When I listened to the stories of survivors sharing their experiences, I came to a decision: Forget the shame, Anita, you must speak up.

Now I go from school to school and before other audiences, speaking to empower students and adults to stand up: "Step in and be a Hero." Remembering is not enough. I have gained a rewarding response in these engagements as audiences pledge not to stay silent in the face of bullies.

I trust my story conveys the immense importance of your presence in safeguarding our future from seeing such horrendous history ever repeat itself.

I look forward to working with Marion on the next book that will address how I survived the tremendous humiliation of the years I have just shared with you in this book. I am hoping that this part of my life will help those who have experienced severe trauma to find the road to their new life.

To find out more go to: AnitaSchorr.com

Words from the writer

As I am writing and reviewing the last pages of this book; I am reflecting on my visit to these dark pages of history.

When I met Anita, I was working on a very different book. Nonetheless, her story and passion inspired me. I decided to put the book I was working on hold and venture on a trip into her past life. I was aware of some of the main events. However, the enormity of the abuse and the devastation it caused, evaded my education. That is when I became zealous about writing her story.

As I visited the past through short passages, Anita could share and I engaged in further research; I uncovered the facts and began to share her passion for the lessons she was imparting to her young listeners as well as the need to pass them on.

In Conclusion: I believe it is important to reflect on the roles that every country played in these devastating actions. Is it out of convenience that we chose to focus on one man and his acolytes? Can the blame be bestowed on one person or country? Let's take as an example, the abandonment of Anita's family by her country of birth, before and after the war.

Marion A. Stahl (marionstahl.com)

"One can always find justifications, but there is never a good reason for cruel treatment."

Book Reading Discussion

Questions:

How does this story illustrate bullying?

How were all the changes in Anita's life possible?

How did Anita react?

What happened to her grandmother?

Could her death have been avoided?

How can I make a difference so that something like this never happens again?

What was happening:

In England?

In the United States?

In Poland?

In Russia?

      In Italy?

      What is a republic?

      What is a monarchy?

      What is a Reich/empire?

      What is the difference?

Why did people still die after the British army came to rescue the prisoners?

What can you/we learn from this book?

Is this possible today?

Why or why not?

Is anything-similar happening today in the world?

Is truth always the best way forward? Anita and her mother lied about Anita not being 18 in order for her to get to the work camp in order to survive.

Czech vocabulary used in this book

bratr – brother

babička – grandmother

miláčku – honey, dear

maminka – mother

Maminko – mom

paštika – pie

Tatinek, páter – father

sestra – sister

Historical highlights of WWII

This is only a partial list of the many events that occurred during this time period. We have compiled dates to aid understanding of the journey of characters in this book.

September 1939

Second Sino-Japanese War. War between Chine and Japan. (Ongoing since October 1938)

1: Japan joins the Axis and China the Allies.

The Invasion of Poland by Nazi Germany begins.

Estonia, Finland, Latvia, Lithuania, Norway, and Switzerland declare their neutrality.

2: The United Kingdom and France issue a joint ultimatum to Germany, requiring German troops to evacuate Polish territory. Italian dictator Benito Mussolini declares the neutrality of his nation. President Douglas Hyde of the Republic of Ireland declares the neutrality of his nation. the Swiss government orders a general mobilization of its forces.

4: The USA launches the Neutrality Patrol.

7: The National Service (Armed Forces) Act 1939 was enacted immediately and enforced full conscription of all males between 18 and 41 resident in the UK.

9: France begins a token offensive, moving into German territory near Saarbrücken.

10: Canada declares war on Germany.

17: The Soviet Union invades Poland from the east.

October 1939

3: British forces move to the Belgian border, anticipating a German invasion of the West.

3: Lithuanians meet Stalin and Molotov in Moscow. Stalin offers Lithuania the city of Vilnius (in Poland) in return for allowing Soviet military bases in Lithuania. The Lithuanians are reluctant.

11: An estimated 158,000 British troops are now in France.

12: Finland's representatives meet Stalin and Molotov in Moscow. Soviet Union demands Finland gives up a military base near Helsinki and exchange some Soviet and Finnish territories to protect Leningrad against Great Britain or the eventual future threat of Germany.

First Soviet forces enter Estonia. During the Umsiedlung, 12,600 Baltic Germans leave Estonia.

19: Portions of Poland are formally inducted into Germany. The first Jewish ghetto is established at Lublin.

November 1939

13: Negotiations between Finland and Soviet Union break down. Finns doubt that Germans and Russians have agreed to include Finland in the Soviet sphere of influence.

14: The Polish government-in-exile moves to London.

16: The first British civilian casualty occurs when a German bomber kills James Isbister in an air raid on Orkney in Scotland.

20: The Luftwaffe and German U-boats begin mining the Thames estuary.

29: The USSR breaks off diplomatic relations with Finland.

30: The Soviet Union attacks Finland in what would become known as the Winter War.

December 1939

14: The USSR is expelled from the League of Nations in response to the Soviet invasion of Finland on November 30.

15: Soviet Army assaulted Taipale, Finland.

18: The first Canadian troops arrive in Europe.

Germany defeats Britain in the Battle of the Heligoland Bight.

January 1940

10: German plane crashes in neutral Belgium. Onboard are the plans for Fall Gelb, these are discovered by the allies, causing a crisis situation.

16: Captured documents reveal Hitler's plans for the invasion of Scandinavia and a postponement of the invasion of France and the Low Countries until the Spring, when the weather is more compatible for an invasion.

17: The Russians are driven back in Finland and retaliate with heavy air attacks.

24: Reinhard Heydrich is appointed by Göring for the solution to "The Jewish question."

27: Germany makes final plans for the invasion of Denmark and Norway.

February 1940

5: Britain and France decide to intervene in Norway to cut off the iron ore trade in anticipation of an expected German occupation and ostensibly to open a route to assist Finland. The operation is scheduled to start about March 20.

10: USSR agrees to supply grain and raw materials to Germany in a new trade treaty.

March 1940

12: In Moscow, Finland signs a peace treaty with the Soviet Union after 105 days of conflict. The Finns are forced to give up significant territory in exchange for independence.

18: Hitler and Mussolini meet at the Brenner pass on the Austrian border. Benito Mussolini agrees with Hitler that Italy will enter the war "at an opportune moment".

21: Paul Reynaud becomes Prime Minister of France following Daladier's resignation the previous day.

28: Britain and France make a formal agreement that neither country will seek a separate peace with Germany.

30: British undertakes secret reconnaissance flights to photograph the targeted areas inside the Soviet Union in preparation for Operation Pike, utilizing high-altitude, high-speed stereoscopic photography pioneered by Sidney Cotton.

April 1940

9: Germans land in several Norwegian ports and take Oslo. The Norwegian campaign lasts two months. The British begin their Norwegian campaign. Denmark surrenders.

10: Germans set up a Norwegian government under Vidkun Quisling, former minister of defense.

12: British troops occupy the Danish Faroe Islands.

14: British and French troops begin landing at Namsos, north of Trondheim in Norway.

May 1940

5: Norwegian government in exile established in London.

10: Germany invades Belgium, France, Luxembourg and the Netherlands. Winston Churchill becomes Prime Minister of the United Kingdom upon the resignation of Neville Chamberlain. The United Kingdom invades Iceland.

The Battle for The Hague become the first failed paratrooper attack in history as the Dutch quickly defeat the invaders.

11: Luxembourg is occupied.

Churchill offers the former Kaiser Wilhelm II, asylum in the United Kingdom but he declines.

12: Battle of Hannut begins in Belgium. The Belgians blow up all the bridges over the Meuse River to halt the German advance.

13: The Dutch fall to the Germans at the Battle of the Grebbeberg.

Dutch government, exile is established in London.

Queen Wilhelmina of the Netherlands flees to asylum in the United Kingdom.

June 1940

9: Red Army provokes conflicts in the Latvian border.

10: Italy declares war on France and the United Kingdom.

13: Paris occupied by German troops. French government moves again, this time to Bordeaux.[2]

16: Philippe Pétain becomes premier of France upon the resignation of Reynaud's government.

17: Soviet troops enter Latvia and Estonia.

18: General De Gaulle forms the Comité français de la Libération nationale, a French government in exile. Estonia, Latvia and Lithuania are occupied by the Soviet Union.

22: Franco-German armistice signed.

24: Franco-Italian armistice signed.

25: France officially surrenders to Germany.

28: General De Gaulle recognized by British as leader of Free French.

The resistance organization founded by Charles de Gaulle in 1940 is in London in order to continue the fight against the Axis powers.

30: Germany invades the Channel Islands.

July 1940

3: The British attack and destroy the French navy, fearing that it would fall into German hands.

4: The destruction of the French Fleet at Mers-el-Kébir, Algeria by the Royal Navy. Vichy French government breaks off diplomatic relations with Britain in protest. At Alexandria the French agree to demilitarize the battleship Lorraine and several smaller ships.

14: Soviets organize rigged elections in the Baltic States. The parliaments will be in the control of the Soviets.

16: Adolf Hitler submits to his military the directive for the invasion of the United Kingdom, Operation Sea Lion.

18: In response to Mers-el-Kébir, the Vichy French Air Force bombs British-held Gibraltar.

August 1940

2: The USSR annexes Bessarabia and Northern Bukovina.

3: The USSR formally annexes Lithuania.

5: The USSR formally annexes Latvia.

6: The USSR formally annexes Estonia.

24:German aircraft mistakenly bomb a church in Cripplegate, accidentally dictating the future shape of the Battle of Britain.

26: Both London and Berlin are bombed, Berlin for the first time.

September 1940

15: Massive German bombing flights on English cities.

16: The Italian invasion of Egypt comes to a halt.

22: The Japanese occupy Vietnam and establish several bases in French Indochina.

27: The Tripartite Pact is signed in Berlin by Germany, Italy, and Japan, promising mutual aid. An informal name, "Axis", emerges.

21: Liverpool is bombed for the 200th time.

25: Berlin and Hamburg are bombed heavily.

28: Italy issues ultimatum to Greece and Greek Prime Minister Metaxas replies: "So it is war". The Italian Royal Army launches attacks into Greece from Italian-held Albania and begins the Greco-Italian War. Hitler is angered at the initiative of his ally.

October 1940

15: Mussolini and his closest advisers decide to invade Greece.

16: Draft registration begins in the United States.

19: The Italians bomb Bahrain.

20: Italian aircraft bomb Cairo, Egypt and American-operated oil refineries in the British Protectorate of Bahrain.

30: President Roosevelt, in the middle of an election campaign, promises not to send "our boys" to war.

November 1940

6-9: British and Indian troops of the Western Desert Force launch Operation Compass, an offensive against Italian forces in Egypt.

18: Hitler issues directive to begin planning for Operation Barbarossa, the German invasion of the Soviet Union.

20: Hungary signs the Tripartite Pact. (see September 27, 1940)

21: The Belgian government, in exile in Britain, declares war on Italy.

23: Romania signs the Tripartite Pact.

24: The Slovak Republic signs the Tripartite Pact.

25: The Soviet Union gives her terms to join the Tripartite Pact including substantial new territorial gains for Russia.

January 1941

10: Lend-Lease introduced into the U.S. Congress. This allowed U.S to provide support.

23: Charles Lindbergh testifies before the U.S. Congress and recommends that the United States negotiate a neutrality pact with Adolf Hitler.

February 1941

15: Deportation of Austrian Jews to ghettos in Poland begins.

20: German and British troops confront each other for the first time in North Africa—at El Agheila in western Libya.

March 1941

1: Hitler gives orders for the expansion of Auschwitz prison camp, to be run by Commandant Rudolf Höss.

8: Another bombing of London, notable because Buckingham Palace is hit.

11: United States President Franklin Delano Roosevelt signs the Lend Lease Act (now passed by the full Congress) allowing Britain, China, and other allied nations to purchase military equipment and to defer payment until after the war.

27: Japanese spy Takeo Yoshikawa arrives in Honolulu, Hawaii and begins to study the United States fleet at Pearl Harbor.

April 1941

1: In Iraq, pro-German Rashid Ali and other members of the "Golden Square" stage a military coup d'état and overthrow the regime of the pro-British Regent 'Abd al-Ilah.

3: A pro-Axis government is installed in Iraq.

10: Greenland is occupied by the United States. With the approval of a "free Denmark", the US will build naval and air bases as counters to the U-boat war.

17: Yugoslavia surrenders. A government in exile is formed in London. King Peter escapes to Greece.

27: Athens is occupied by German troops. Greece surrenders.

27: Athens is occupied by German troops. Greece surrenders.

May 1941

15: First Civilian Public Service camp opens for conscientious objectors in the United States.

224

21: The US merchantman SS Robin Moor is sunk by German submarine U-69. The incident startles the nation, and President Roosevelt shortly announces an "unlimited national emergency."

June 1941

16: All German and Italian consulates in the United States are ordered closed and their staffs to leave the country by July 10.

22: Germany invades the Soviet Union with Operation Barbarossa, a three-pronged operation aimed at Leningrad, Moscow, and the southern oil fields of the Caucasus. Romania invades southern Russia on the side of Germany.

With full Finnish consent, German troops begin deploying in formally neutral Finnish territory, to attack the Soviet Union from there.

28: Italian-occupied Albania declares war on the Soviet Union. : Huge German encirclement of 300,000 Red Army troops near Minsk and Białystok.

29: Finish and German troops begin Operation Arctic Fox against the Soviet Union.

July 1941

4: Mass murder of Polish scientists and writers, committed by German troops in captured Polish city of Lwów.

7: British and Canadian troops in Iceland are replaced by Americans.

15: Argentina naval air base is set up in Newfoundland. It will prove an important transfer station for the Allies for some years.

19: The "V-sign", displayed most notably by Churchill, is unofficially adopted as the Allied signal, along with the motif of Beethoven's Fifth Symphony.

26: In response to the Japanese occupation of French Indochina, US President Franklin D. Roosevelt orders the seizure of all Japanese assets in the United States.

31: The Japanese naval ministry accuses the United States of intruding into their territorial waters at Sukumo Bay, and then fleeing. No evidence is offered to prove this allegation.

August 1941

1: The US announces an oil embargo against "aggressors."

1: Japanese occupy Saigon, Vietnam.

28: German forces with the help of Estonian volunteers take Tallinn from Soviets.

September 1941

11: Franklin D. Roosevelt orders the United States Navy to shoot on sight if any ship or convoy is threatened.

28: German SS troops kill over 30,000 Jews at Babi Yar on the outskirts of Kiev, Ukraine, in response to sabotage efforts which the Germans attributed to local Jews .26: The US Naval Command orders an all-out war on Axis shipping in American waters.

30: President Roosevelt approves US$1 billion in Lend-Lease aid to the Soviet Union.

December 1941

4: Japanese naval and army forces continue to move toward Pearl Harbor and South-east Asia.

6: UK declares war on Finland.

7: Japan launches an attack on Pearl Harbor, declares war on the United States and the United Kingdom and invades Thailand and British Malaya and launches aerial attacks against Guam, Hong Kong, the Philippines, Shanghai, Singapore and Wake Island. (December 8, Asian time zones)

Japan declares war on the UK and the USA.

Canada declares war on Japan.

German "Night and Fog decree" dictates the elimination of anti-Nazis in Western Europe.

8: The United States, the United Kingdom, the Netherlands and New Zealand declare war on Japan.

9: China and Australia officially declare war on Japan.

17: Battle of Sevastopol begins.

19: Hitler becomes Supreme Commander-in-Chief of the German Army.

30: The first "Liberty Ship", the SS Patrick Henry is launched. Liberty Ships will prove to be major parts of the Allied supply system.

January 1942

1: Twenty-six Allied countries signed the Declaration by United Nations during the Arcadia Conference.

10: Japan declares war on the Netherlands.

11: Japanese troops capture Kuala Lumpur, Malaya.

15: German authorities begin to deport Jews from the Lodz ghettos to the Chelmno Concentration Camp.

26: The first American forces arrive in Europe, landing in Northern Ireland.

February 1942

19: Japanese aircraft attack Darwin, in Australia's Northern Territory.

19: President Franklin D. Roosevelt signs Executive Order 9066 allowing the United States military to define areas as exclusionary zones. These zones affect the Japanese on the West Coast, and Germans and Italians primarily on the East Coast.

25: The internment of Japanese-American citizens in the Western United States begins as fears of invasion increase.

March 1942

3: Japanese aircraft make a surprising raid on the airfield and harbour at Broome, Western Australia.

5: The Japanese capture Batavia, the capital of the Dutch East Indies.

26: Jews in Berlin must now clearly identify their houses.

May 1942

15: In the United States, a bill creating the Women's Auxiliary Army Corps (WAAC) is signed into law.

20: The first African-American seamen are taken into the United States Navy.

June 1942

1: First reports in the West that gas is being used to kill the Jews sent to "the East".

18: Manhattan Project is started, the beginning of a scientific approach to nuclear weapons.

18: Winston Churchill arrives in Washington for meetings with Roosevelt.

July 1942

4: First air missions by American Air Force in Europe.

6: Vel' d'Hiv Roundup: On order from the Vichy France government headed by Pierre Laval, French police officers arrest 13,152 Jews and hold them at the Winter Velodrome before deportation to Auschwitz.

22: The systematic deportation of Jews from the Warsaw Ghetto begins. Treblinka, "a model" concentration camp, is opened in Poland.

August 1942

11-15: The Operation Pedestal takes place: British operation to get desperately needed supplies to the island of Malta in August 1942.

September 1942

September is marked by many shipwrecks.

October 1942

11: Battle of Cape Esperance - On the Northwest coast of Guadalcanal, United States Navy ships intercept and defeat a Japanese fleet on their way to reinforce troops on the island. With the help of radar they sink one cruiser and several Japanese destroyers.

29: In the United Kingdom, leading clergymen and political figures hold a public meeting to register outrage over Nazi Germany's persecution of Jews.

November 1942

1: The Americans begin the Matanikau Offensive against the Japanese.

December 1942

7: On the anniversary of the Pearl Harbor attack, the USS New Jersey, America's largest battleship is launched (commissioned five months later).

January 1943

16: Iraq declares war on the Axis powers.

18: Prisoners in the Warsaw Ghetto rise up for the first time, starting the Warsaw Ghetto Uprising.

February 1943

5: The Allies now have all of Libya under control.

March 1943

1: Battle of the Bismarck Sea. U.S. and Australian naval forces, over the course of three days, sink eight Japanese troop transports near New Guinea.

13: German forces liquidate the Jewish ghetto in Kraków.

14: Germans recapture Kharkov.

23: American tanks defeat the Germans at El Guettar, Tunisia.

April 1943

15: Finland officially rejects Soviet terms for peace.

May 1943

15: The French form a "Resistance Movement."

16: The Warsaw Ghetto Uprising ends. The ghetto has been destroyed, with about 14,000 Jews killed and about another 40,000 sent to the death camp at Treblinka.

22: Allies bomb Sicily and Sardinia, both potential landing sites.

July 1943

11: Ukrainian Insurgent Army massacres Poles at Dominopol.

22: U.S. forces under Patton capture Palermo, Sicily.

August 1943

6: German troops start pouring in to take over Italy's defenses.

September 1943

10: German troops occupy Rome. The Italian fleet meanwhile surrenders at Malta and other Mediterranean ports.

11: British troops enter Bari in southeastern Italy.

28: The people of Naples, sensing the approach of the Allies, rise up against the German occupiers.

30: With the Gestapo starting to round up Danish Jews, certain Danes are secretly sending their Jewish countrymen to Sweden by means of dangerous boat crossings.

October 1943

4: Corsica is liberated by Free French forces.

13: Italy declares war on Germany.

November 1943

5: The Italians bomb the Vatican in a failed attempt to knock out the Vatican radio.

9: General De Gaulle becomes President of the French Committee of National Liberation.

16: 160 American bombers strike a hydro-electric power facility and heavy water factory in German-controlled Vemork, Norway.

22: The Cairo Conference: US President Franklin D. Roosevelt, British Prime Minister Winston Churchill, and Chinese leader Chiang Kai-Shek meet in Cairo, Egypt, to discuss ways to defeat Japan.

27: Huge civilian losses in Berlin as heavy bombing raids continue.

December 1943

13: German soldiers carry out the Massacre of Kalavryta in southern Greece.

14: United States XV Corps arrives in European Theater.

24: US General Dwight D. Eisenhower becomes the Supreme Allied Commander in Europe.

26: German battleship Scharnhorst is sunk off North Cape (in the Arctic) by an array of British cruisers and destroyer torpedoes.

February 1944

8: The plan for the invasion of France, Operation Overlord, is confirmed.

The 1st Ukrainian Front of the Red Army enters Poland.

19: Leipzig, Germany is bombed for two straight nights. This marks the beginning of a "Big Week" bombing campaign against German industrial cities by Allied bombers.

March 1944

15: The National Council of the French Resistance approves the Resistance program.

17: Heavy bombing of Vienna.

18: German forces occupy Hungary. The Red Army approach Romanian border.

April 1944

4: General Charles de Gaulle takes command of all Free French forces.

17: Japanese launch a major offensive in central China.

21: An Allied air raid on Paris kills a large number of civilians.

May 1944

6: Heavy Allied bombings of the Continent in preparation for D-Day.

8: D-Day for Operation Overlord set for June 5.

21: Increased Allied bombing of targets in France in preparation for D-Day.

23: Allies advance toward Rome, after a linkup of American II and III corps.

25: Germans are now in retreat in the Anzio area.

June 1944

2: The provisional French government is established.

3: There are daily bombings of the Cherbourg peninsula and the Normandy area.

4: Operation Overlord is postponed 24 hours due to high seas.

5: Rome falls to the Allies, becoming the first capital of an Axis nation to do so.

Operation Overlord commences when more than 1,000 British bombers drop 5,000 tons of bombs on German gun batteries on the Normandy coast in preparation for D-Day. And the first Allied troops land in Normandy. Paratroopers are scattered from Caen southward.

6: D-Day begins with the landing of 155,000 Allied troops on the beaches of Normandy in France. The allied soldiers quickly break through the Atlantic Wall and push inland in the largest amphibious military operation in history.

July 1944

7: Soviet troops enter Vilnius, Lithuania.

August 1944

4: Florence is liberated by the Allies, particularly British and South African troops

Rennes, is liberated by American forces.

15: The Allies reach the "Gothic Line", the last German strategic position in North Italy.

16: The Red Armies makes moves to close in on Warsaw.

19: French Resistance begins uprising in Paris, partly inspired by the Allied approach to the Seine River.

25: Paris is liberated. De Gaulle and the Free French parade triumphantly down the Champs-Élysées.

28: The Germans surrender at Toulon and Marseilles, in southern France.

31: The Soviet army enters Bucharest.

American forces turn over the government of France to Free French troops.

September 1944

1: Canadian troops capture Dieppe, France.

2: Allied troops enter Belgium. 2: Finland agrees to an armistice with the Soviet Union and demands a withdrawal of German troops.

10: Luxembourg is liberated by U.S. First Army.

22: The Red Army takes Tallinn, the first Baltic harbor outside the minefields of the Gulf of Finland.

October 1944

1: Soviet troops enter Yugoslavia.

2: American troops are now in a full-scale attack on the German "West Wall".

November 1944

5: Zionist terrorists assassinate the British government representative in the Middle East.

6: Franklin Delano Roosevelt wins a fourth term.

January 1945

2: The Japanese increasingly use kamikaze tactics against the US naval forces nearby.

8: The battle of Strasbourg is underway, with Americans in defense of their recent acquisition.

13: The Battle of Budapest ends with Soviet victory, after a long defense by the Germans.

20: The Red Army advances into East Prussia. Germans renew the retreat.

24: Egypt declares war on the Axis.

Massive bombing of Germany by approximately 9,000 bombers.

25: Turkey declares war on Germany.

26: Syria declares war on Germany and Japan.

March 1945

4: Bratislava, the capital of the Slovak Republic, is overrun by advancing Soviet forces.

31: General Eisenhower broadcasts a demand for the Germans to surrender.

April 1945

10: Buchenwald concentration camp liberated by American forces.

19: Switzerland closes its borders with Germany (and former Austria).

20: Hitler celebrates his 56th birthday in the bunker in Berlin. Reports are that he is in an unhealthy state, nervous, and depressed.

27: The encirclement of German forces in Berlin is completed by the 1st Belorussian Front and the 1st Ukrainian Front.

29: Dachau concentration camp is liberated by the U.S. 7th Army. All forces in Italy officially surrender and a ceasefire is declared.

Hitler marries his companion Eva Braun.

30: Hitler and his wife commit suicide, he by a combination of poison and a gunshot. Before he dies Adolf Hitler dictates his last will and testament. In it Joseph Goebbels is appointed Reich Chancellor and Grand Admiral Karl Dönitz is appointed Reich President.

15: Bergen-Belsen concentration camp is liberated by the British Army.

May 1945

2: The Battle of Berlin ends when German General Helmuth Weidling, commander of the Berlin Defense Area, unconditionally surrenders the city of Berlin to Soviet General Vasily Chuikov.

8: Prague uprising ends with negotiated surrender with Czech resistance. This allowed the Germans in Prague to leave the city.

11: Prague offensive ends with Soviet capture of the capital city, the last major city to be liberated, though the war is over. Eisenhower stops Patton from participating in the liberation.

11: German Army Group Centre in Czechoslovakia surrenders.

Sources: Wikipedia: World War II

11: Prague offensive ends with Soviet capture of the capital city, the last major city to be liberated, though the war is over. Eisenhower stops Patton from participating in the liberation.

11: German Army Group Centre in Czechoslovakia surrenders.

Sources: Wikipedia: World War II

References:

(1)   See history of Czechoslovakia in addendum
(2)   Wikipedia: Brno Exibition Center.
(3)   Tugendhat. (tugendhat.eu)
(4)   Wikipedia: Ludwig Mies van der Robe.
(5)   Day ensemble, ca. 1927. The Metropolitan Museum of Art, Costume Institute. 1984.31a–c
(6) Wikipedia: Spilberk Castle

(1) Wikipedia: League of Nation Accesses 7/26/13

(2) "Covenant of the League of Nations" The Avalon Project. Retrieved 30 August 2011.

(7) **Sudenten German**. *The German speaking regions according to mother tongue popularly referred to in interwar period as the Sudetenland.*
   Sudenten Crisis: *The Munich Agreement was a settlement permitting Nazi Germany's annexation of Czechoslovakia's areas along the country's borders mainly inhabited by German speakers, for which a new territorial designation "Sudetenland" was coined.*
 (8) Czechoslovak Constitution of

(9)   Quote by Winston Churchill.
(10) **Skoda**: *Škoda Auto go back to the early 1890s. During the World War II Occupation of Czechoslovakia, the Škoda works was turned into part of Reichswerke Hermann Göring serving the German World War II effort. Škoda is located in Plzen, Czech Republic.*
(11) Plzen: The City of Plzen, former Capital of West Moravia, became the center for industrial growth. Germany wanted a hold of the town because of it's

important resources.
(12) Republic: A republic is a form of government in which affairs of state are a "public matter See Definition addendum #11.

(13) **Tomáš Garrigue Masaryk:** *Founder and first President of Czechoslovakia. See Definition addendum #11.*
(14) **Kristallnacht**: *Literally, "Night of Crystal," is often referred to as the "Night of Broken Glass." See Definition addendum #11.*
(15) See Sudetenland crisis in Addendum (02)
(16) See Sudetenland crisis in Addendum (02)
(17) German occupation of Czechoslovakia (1938–1945) See Addentum #2
(18) Following the Anschluss (annexation) of Nazi Germany and Austria, in March 1938, the conquest of Czechoslovakia became Hitler's next ambition. The incorporation of the Sudetenland into Nazi Germany left the rest of Czechoslovakia weak and it became powerless to resist subsequent occupation. On 16 March 1939, the German moved into Prague Castle, and later that fall Brno. Hitler proclaimed Bohemia and Moravia the Protectorate of Bohemia and Moravia. (Spencer Tucker, Priscilla Mary Roberts (2005). World War II: A Political, Social, and Military History. ABC-CLIO. ISBN 1-57607-999-6.)
(19) League of Nation. Also of interest are the "Fourteen Points". Wikipedia Accesses 7/26/13
(20) "Covenant of the League of Nations" The Avalon Project. Retrieved 30 August 2011.
(22) Berlin Diary by William Shirer by acclaimed journalist and bestselling author of The Rise and Fall of the Third Reich, this day-by-day, eyewitness account of the momentous events leading up to World War II in Europe.
(23) Kellogg-Briand Pact. (http://history.state.gov)
(23-b) History Place, published by Philip Gavin.
(24) Czech resistance to Nazi occupation. From Wikipedia, accessed 7/30/13.
(25) The Jewish population in Brno. See addendum # 5.

Transport History and resources. Source: Geni.com See
Addendum #5. Yad Vashem, Transport database.
(26) History of Brno Jewish community. See addendum.
(27) Wikipedia: The Slovak Republic and the Holocaust
(accessed 7/12/13)
(28) Ghetto: A ghetto is a term, often referred to as a
part of a city in which members of a minority group live,
especially because of social, legal, or economic
pressure. See Addendum # 11
(29) Wikipedia: Jakob Edelstein
(30) **Yeshiva:** Yeshiva is a Jewish educational
institution.
(32) Tsukunft or Cukunft or Zukunft (Yiddish for future)
was the youth organization of the General Jewish Labor
Union (or Bund). See Addendum # 11.
(33) Zionist versus Bund: See Addendum # 11.
 (34) Building a New Society: Bund
(34) Wikipedia; Herschel Grynszpan
(35)   Paradise Camp; See resources and addendum
Therezin: and Addendum # 11 Terezin Definition. Little
Fortress and large Fortress.
(36)   Ghetto   Police   A Czech Special   Department-
Gendarmerie
(37)   Brundibár is a children's opera by Jewish Czech
          composer Hans Krása with a libretto by Adolf
          Hoffmeister, originally performed by the children
          of Theresienstadt concentration camp in occupied
          Czechoslovakia. The name comes from a Czech
          colloquialism for a bumblebee.
(38)   Yivo Encyclopedia of Jews in Eastern Europe.
(39)   "A Boy in Terezín", The Private Diary of Pavel
          Weiner, April 1944-April 1945
(40)   Rafael Schächter. He formed a chorus within the
          camp and gave a performance of the massive and
          complex Requiem by Giuseppe
          Verdi. Schächter would   go   on   to   conduct
          fifteenmore performances of the work before his
          eventual deportation to Auschwitz-Birkenau

(41)   Friedl Dicker-Brandeis: Artist   and   art teacher Friedl Dicker-Brandeis created drawing classes for children in the ghetto to whom she also taught Hana Brady (Hana's suitcase). This activity resulted in the production of over four thousand children's drawings, which Dicker-Brandeis hid in two suitcases before being sent to Auschwitz.

(42)   Nazi   Medical   ExperimentsS.   US   Holocaust Memorial Museum.

Hepatitis Experiments: PMID: 2698560 [PubMed

(43)   The   GPO.   General   Plan   Ost   (GPO)   (English: Master Plan East) was a secret Nazi German plan for the colonization of Central   and   Eastern   Europe. Implementing   it   would   have necessitated genocide and ethnic cleansing on a vast scale to be undertaken in these European territories occupied by Germany during World War II.

(44)   Ein   Dokumentarfilm   aus   dem   jüdischen Siedlungsgebiet, The Fuhrer Gives the Jews a City. (Archive.org). This film is about a concentrated place in a Czechoslovakian city named Theresienstadt, given to the Jews for preparations to deport them to either Israel or Madagascar.

(45) The Maccabi World Union is an international Jewish sports organization spanning five continents and more than fifty countries, with some 400,000 members. Maccabi World Union organizes the Maccabiah Games, a prominent international Jewish athletics event. The Maccabi World Union was created at the 12th World Jewish Congress in Karlovy Vary, Czechoslovakia in 1921. It was then decided by the secretariat of Jewish sport leaders to form one umbrella organization for all Jewish sports associations. Its aims were defined as working "foster physical education, belief in Jewish heritage and the Jewish nation, and to work actively for the rebuilding of our own country and for the preservation of our people". In 1960, the International Olympic Committee officially recognized the Maccabi World Union as an "Organization of Olympic Standing".)

(46)   See History Addendum: US position.

(47)   Camp Uniform and Procedures:
The different types of clothing used as prisoners' attire in the Auschwitz camps relate mainly to the time/period when each prisoner arrived at the camp. Only two categories of prisoners were allowed to wear their own civilian clothes in Auschwitz and not have their heads shaved. The first were the inmates from the Theresienstadt ghetto in Czechoslovakia who were transported to the so-called Theresienstadt Familienlager (the Terezín Family Camp) in the Auschwitz-Birkenau sector BIIb, a camp section established for Nazi propaganda purposes.
Source: Historical, Sociological and Methodological approach 2010, By Sofia Pantouvaki (b)
        (a) Testimony of Jerzy Adan Brandhuber, APMAB, 166257/2264 in Collections of Testimonies, vol. 95.
        (b) See S. Pantouvaki (2008: 219-220) and V. Blodig (2003:113).

Marion A. Stahl

(48) The Terezín Family Camp in Auschwitz-Birkenau sector BIIb was created with the intention of misleading the public with respect to the treatment of the Jews. The inmates destined to be sent to the Family Camp did not go through the selection procedure upon arrival in Auschwitz. Also, several child survivors from the Terezín Family Camp testify to this fact, i.e. Dagmar Lieblová (born Fantlová), Evelina Merová (born Landová), interviews with S. Pantouvaki, 21 and 19 September 2009 respectively. As far as footwear is concerned, the prisoners received one of the following three types: either Dutch-type wooden shoe-like clogs made of one piece of wood, called Holländer ("Dutchman" clogs); or clogs with leather uppers (a wooden bottom with a scrap of tarpaulin on top suspended by the foot); these were called Holzpantinen (wooden clogs). The third type was a shoe made of a wooden bottom and a tarpaulin upper, covering most of the foot and reinforced with scraps of leather; these were called Holzschulen (wooden shoes). These were the assorted shoe types produced especially for the Nazi concentration camps.

When prisoners were exterminated at Auschwitz, not only their clothing, but also their shoes were issued to other inmates.

Probably, the most well known aspect of concentration camp prisoner identification relates to the insignia used to indicate each specific "category" of prisoners. Precise identification symbols were added to the striped clothing: Triangle stars, as well as letters and dots in specific colors symbolizing the category the prisoner belonged to (i.e. Nationality, Jews, Jehovah's Witnesses and clergy, political prisoners, common criminals, delinquents, homosexuals or any other particular group, such as escape-prone prisoners).

(48b) Adapted from "I Promise To Come Back" written and Illustrated by Shira Underberger. A student who had heard Anuta's story and made a children's book.

From Wikipedia. Forced labor under German rule during World War II, accessed 7/12/13.

(49) Panikos Panayi, "Exploitation, Criminality, Resistance. The Everyday Life of Foreign Workers and Prisoners of War in the German Town of Osnabrück, 1939-49," Journal of Contemporary History Vol. 40, No. 3 (Jul., 2005), pp. 483-502 in JSTOR.
From Wikipedia. Battle of Hamburg, accessed 7/12/13.
(50) "The Cabinet Papers 1915–1978: Glossary - B". The National Archives. Retrieved 2009-06-10.
(51) "The Forgotten Holocaust", by Richard C. Lukas, The University Press of Kentucky and "The Jews and the Poles in World War II" by Stefan Korbonski, Hippocrene Books.
(52) In Neugraben was a subcamp of the Nazi concentration camp Neuengamme. On September 13, 1944 the women's subcamp was opened in Falkenbergweg. 500 Czechish-Jewish women coming from the Ghetto Theresienstadt were deported to the Auschwitz concentration camp. The SS in Auschwitz selected the women for labor in Hamburg. In the Neugraben camp the work was building auxiliary homes, also laying supply pipes and building streets in the neighborhood Falkenbergsiedlung.
During the last months of World War II, some of the women had to do clearing up work in Hamburg's oil industry and to dig antitank obstacles in Hamburg-Hausbruch.
(53) In February 1945, the SS transferred the women to the camp Hamburg-Tiefstack and later from there to the Bergen-Belsen concentration camp.
(54) Klinkerwerk (brick factory) of the DEST
From: http://www.kz-gedenkstaette-neuengamme.de
(55) Tattoos and numbers: The System of identifying prisoners at Auschwitz. (http://www.ushmm.org)
(56) Mark Weber, historian and author, is director of the Institute for Historical Review. Encyclopaedia Judaica, Vol. 4, p. 610; Gedenkbuch: Opfer der Verfolgung der Juden unter der nationsozialistischen Gewaltherrschaft (Koblenz: Bundesarchiv, 1986; 2 vols.), pp. 1761-1762
(57) http://www.bergenbelsen.co.uk

Marion A. Stahl

(58)   From Wikipedia. Forced labor under German
rule during World War II, accessed 7/12/13
(59)   U.S. Holocaust Memorial Museum; Encyclopedia
Britannica;   Simon   Wiesenthal   Center   Multimedia
Learning Center Online; Georgia Tech Library; United
States Holocaust Memorial Museum; "Rebirth after the
Holocaust: The Bergen-Belsen Displaced Persons Camp,
1945-1950."

Marion A. Stahl

Book Reviews:

Excellent
Not only does this book cover atrocities and "events" on a grand scale, it also covers repugnant atrocities of a family. EVERYONE should read this well-done history.
By **Steven Bouchard**

Page-turning memoir
Admittedly, memoirs aren't my favorite, but I do read them and this one is wonderful. I really liked how the author brought in trivia and historical points, as both a comparison and a timeline tool for the reader. The historical aspects were engrossing and her storyteller style made the combination of history and Anita's story, seamless. The photos are a charming addition to the story and the recipes reminded me of my grandmother.
The story engages you from the onset as we feel the worry and loss of Anita while she searches for her family. We also feel the camaraderie of her and her friends as they gossip about boys and what they want in life. Anita is like many teen girls forced to grow up too quickly in a world at war.
By **Leslie Obrien**

First hand account of a child in a concentration camp from beginning to the end
I was reminded quickly how life and family dynamics can change from stable and loving to chaotic and uncertain. Author Marion A. Stahl did a wonderful job engaging the reader on Anita's evacuation and several moves with other Jews that would ultimately lead to family separation and a concentration camp.

You may discover in part as I did, that the human optimistic will to survive may be the most important ingredient in trauma. With family suicide being a choice for some, it was March 23, 1943 where the day of transport began and where home no longer existed. In detailed fashion will events capture and enrage you on

249

how such injustices were allowed and carried out by those indifferent to human suffering.

Though a melancholy plot, there is a hope that has sprung from the ashes of life as today she lives to speak to audiences, empowering them.

This book is history at its finest as you will gain the inside picture into both event and emotions. Sometimes in life losses can ultimately be gains in other avenues. I recommend this book with a 5-star rating as the contents will captivate you page after page.
By **Valerie Caraotta** (CONYERS, GA, US)

Historical Reality for ALL Ages-Well-Written, Moving, Powerful

If Be a Hero: A Witness to History doesn't burrow into your heart and mind, I can't imagine what will. This is powerful reading, moving, educational and the true story of a young girl who survived.

What kept Anita going, how was she able to survive? Was it holding on to the happy memories, love of family and the way life used to be? Was it an inner strength and resourcefulness? Anita's story comes to life under the pen of Marion A. Stahl, chronicling Anita's life before the German invasion and after the hateful and horrendous devastation of their occupation.

As an educational tool, no student should miss Anita's story. This is history, the proof of the cruelties that racism and bullying, greed and the lust for power can create. Much more personal than a classic textbook, Be a Hero: Anita's Piano allows the reader to see, hear and feel the truth of living through such atrocities. It takes a caring hand to write this tale and a brave soul to share their life with such honesty. I cannot recommend this book enough to ALL readers, young and not so young.
By **Dii** (Florida)

Anita Pollakova is a hero because she survived in spite of the degradation, brutality, humility, and inhuman

horrors she, her family and others were subjected to through no fault of their own, but because a madman wanted to conquer to world.
By **Elena Dorothy Bowman** (Massachusetts)

A Poignant, Intimate Portrait of the Holocaust through the Lens of Family

Marion A. Stahl writes with rare vision and inspiration, bringing readers the story of the Holocaust through the lens of family. We meet Anita as a young child, amidst her idyllic life of home, family, and community. But as Hitler's influence grows, the very fabric of their lives begins to unravel as one by one, the family is pulled apart. Anita finds the courage to navigate her changing world and is determined to find her family, to reunite the pieces she has lost.

Marion manages to write with such a fresh and authentic voice, that I felt completely transported, as if I were viewing the Holocaust's infamous events for the first time.
By **thepaigeduke** (Texas)

A Child's View of the Holocaust - Chilling, but Essential Reading

Stahl's book is intended as a discussion tool to introduce students to the Holocaust. It is just as valuable for any reader seeking a better understanding of how madness can spread so quickly and lead to such catastrophic results – how otherwise decent people can take part in, or ignore, unimaginable cruelty.
By **Charles Ray** (North Potomac, Maryland, United States)

A Good Book for Everyone To Read

I think Anita's story, as written by Marion Stahl, should be required reading for students in schools to remind children and adults alike that humans have the capacity to be the worst they can possibly be when they act out of hatred, and they have the capacity to be the best they can be when they act out of love and caring, and that it's important for each of us to choose the latter.
By **Kirsten OConnor**

`You can make a difference. Step in and be a hero.'

This book is as much a scrapbook as it is a memoir of a heroic woman: it is filled with photographs of family, of furniture, maps, documents, recipes, places, and other memorabilia that help bring to light the life of the amazing Anita Ron Schorr - her life as a child of a well to do, musical family in Brno, Czechoslovakia during the 1930s and 1940s as the heinous flame of Adolph Hitler consumed Europe and threatened the world. The core spirit of this book is profoundly moving.
By **Gardy Harp**

To read more about Anita or listen to her today go to: AnitaSchorr.com

References:

(6)   See history of Czechoslovakia in addendum
(7)   Wikipedia: Brno Exibition Center.
(8)   Tugendhat. (tugendhat.eu)
(9)   Wikipedia: Ludwig Mies van der Robe.
(10)   Day ensemble, ca. 1927. The Metropolitan Museum of Art, Costume Institute. 1984.31a–c
(6) Wikipedia: Spilberk Castle

(3) Wikipedia: League of Nation Accesses 7/26/13

(4) "Covenant of the League of Nations" The Avalon Project. Retrieved 30 August 2011.

(7) **Sudenten German**. *The German speaking regions according to mother tongue popularly referred to in interwar period as the Sudetenland.*

Sudenten Crisis: *The Munich Agreement was a settlement permitting Nazi Germany's annexation of Czechoslovakia's areas along the country's borders mainly inhabited by German speakers, for which a new territorial designation "Sudetenland" was coined.*
(8) Czechoslovak Constitution of

(9) Quote by Winston Churchill.
(10) **Skoda**: *Škoda Auto go back to the early 1890s. During the World War II Occupation of Czechoslovakia, the Škoda works was turned into part of Reichswerke Hermann Göring serving the German World War II effort. Škoda is located in Plzen, Czech Republic.*

(11) *Plzen: The City of Plzen, former Capital of West Moravia, became the center for industrial growth. Germany wanted a hold of the town because of it's important resources.*

(12) *Republic: A republic is a form of government in which affairs of state are a "public matter See Definition addendum #11.*

(13) **Tomáš Garrigue Masaryk:** *Founder and first President of Czechoslovakia. See Definition addendum #11.*

(14) **Kristallnacht**: *Literally, "Night of Crystal," is often referred to as the "Night of Broken Glass." See Definition addendum #11.*

(15) *See Sudetenland crisis in Addendum (02)*

(16) *See Sudetenland crisis in Addendum (02)*

(17) *German occupation of Czechoslovakia (1938–1945) See Addentum #2*

(18) *Following the Anschluss (annexation) of Nazi Germany and Austria, in March 1938, the conquest of Czechoslovakia became Hitler's next ambition. The incorporation of the Sudetenland into Nazi Germany left the rest of Czechoslovakia weak and it became powerless to resist subsequent occupation. On 16 March 1939, the German moved into Prague Castle, and later that fall Brno. Hitler proclaimed Bohemia and Moravia the Protectorate of Bohemia and Moravia. (Spencer Tucker, Priscilla Mary Roberts (2005). World War II: A Political, Social, and Military History. ABC-CLIO. ISBN 1-57607-999-6.)*

(19) *League of Nation. Also of interest are the "Fourteen Points". Wikipedia Accesses 7/26/13*

(20) *"Covenant of the League of Nations" The Avalon Project. Retrieved 30 August 2011.*

(22) *Berlin Diary by William Shirer by acclaimed journalist and bestselling author of The Rise and Fall of the Third Reich, this day-by-day, eyewitness account of the momentous events leading up to World War II in Europe.*

(23) Kellogg-Briand Pact. (http://history.state.gov)

(23-b) History Place, published by Philip Gavin.

(24) Czech resistance to Nazi occupation. From Wikipedia, accessed 7/30/13.

(25) The Jewish population in Brno. See addendum # 5. Transport History and resources. Source: Geni.com See Addendum #5. Yad Vashem, Transport database.

(26) History of Brno Jewish community. See addendum.

(27) Wikipedia: The Slovak Republic and the Holocaust (accessed 7/12/13)

(28) Ghetto: A ghetto is a term, often referred to as a part of a city in which members of a minority group live, especially because of social, legal, or economic pressure. See Addendum # 11

(29) Wikipedia: Jakob Edelstein

(30) **Yeshiva:** *Yeshiva is a Jewish educational institution.*

(32) Tsukunft or Cukunft or Zukunft (Yiddish for future) was the youth organization of the General Jewish Labor Union (or Bund). See Addendum # 11.

(33) Zionist versus Bund: See Addendum # 11.

(34) Building a New Society: Bund

(34) Wikipedia; Herschel Grynszpan

(35) Paradise Camp; See resources and addendum Therezin: and Addendum # 11 Terezin Definition. Little Fortress and large Fortress.

(36) Ghetto Police A Czech Special Department-Gendarmerie

(37) Brundibár is a children's opera by Jewish Czech composer Hans Krása with a libretto by Adolf Hoffmeister, originally performed by the children of Theresienstadt concentration camp in occupied Czechoslovakia. The name comes from a Czech colloquialism for a bumblebee.

(38) Yivo Encyclopedia of Jews in Eastern Europe.

(39) "A Boy in Terezín", The Private Diary of Pavel Weiner, April 1944-April 1945

(40)   *Rafael Schächter. He formed a chorus within the camp and gave a performance of the massive and complex Requiem by Giuseppe Verdi. Schächter would go on to conduct fifteen more performances of the work before his eventual deportation to Auschwitz-Birkenau*

(41)   *Friedl Dicker-Brandeis: Artist   and   art teacher Friedl Dicker-Brandeis created drawing classes for children in the ghetto to whom she also taught Hana Brady (Hana's suitcase). This activity resulted in the production of over four thousand children's drawings, which Dicker-Brandeis hid in two suitcases before being sent to Auschwitz.*

(42)   *Nazi Medical ExperimentsS. US Holocaust Memorial Museum.*

Hepatitis Experiments: PMID: 2698560 [PubMed

(43)   *The GPO. General Plan Ost (GPO) (English: Master Plan East) was a secret Nazi German plan for the colonization of Central and Eastern Europe. Implementing it would have necessitated genocide and ethnic cleansing on a vast scale to be undertaken in these European territories occupied by Germany during World War II.*

(44)   *Ein Dokumentarfilm aus dem jüdischen Siedlungsgebiet, The Fuhrer Gives the Jews a City. (Archive.org). This film is about a concentrated place in a Czechoslovakian city named Theresienstadt, given to the Jews for preparations to deport them to either Israel or Madagascar.*

(45) The Maccabi World Union is an international Jewish sports organization spanning five continents and more than fifty countries, with some 400,000 members. Maccabi World Union organizes the Maccabiah Games, a prominent international Jewish athletics event. The Maccabi World Union was created at the 12th World Jewish Congress in Karlovy Vary, Czechoslovakia in 1921. It was then decided by the secretariat of Jewish sport leaders to form one umbrella organization for all Jewish sports associations. Its aims were defined as working "foster physical education, belief in Jewish heritage and the Jewish nation, and to work actively for the rebuilding of our own country and for the preservation of our people". In 1960, the International Olympic Committee officially recognized the Maccabi World Union as an "Organization of Olympic Standing".)

(46)   See History Addendum: US position.

(47)   Camp Uniform and Procedures:
The different types of clothing used as prisoners' attire in the Auschwitz camps relate mainly to the time/period when each prisoner arrived at the camp. Only two categories of prisoners were allowed to wear their own civilian clothes in Auschwitz and not have their heads shaved. The first were the inmates from the Theresienstadt ghetto in Czechoslovakia who were transported to the so-called Theresienstadt Familien-lager (the Terezín Family Camp) in the Auschwitz-Birkenau sector BIIb, a camp section established for Nazi propaganda purposes.
Source: Historical, Sociological and Methodological approach 2010, By Sofia Pantouvaki (b)
*   (a) Testimony of Jerzy Adan Brandhuber, APMAB, 166257/2264 in Collections of Testimonies, vol. 95.*
*   (b) See S. Pantouvaki (2008: 219-220) and V. Blodig (2003:113).*

(48) The Terezín Family Camp in Auschwitz-Birkenau sector BIIb was created with the intention of misleading the public with respect to the treatment of the Jews. The inmates destined to be sent to the Family Camp did not go through the selection procedure upon arrival in Auschwitz. Also, several child survivors from the Terezín Family Camp testify to this fact, i.e. Dagmar Lieblová (born Fantlová), Evelina Merová (born Landová), interviews with S. Pantouvaki, 21 and 19 September 2009 respectively. As far as footwear is concerned, the prisoners received one of the following three types: either Dutch-type wooden shoe-like clogs made of one piece of wood, called Holländer ("Dutchman" clogs); or clogs with leather uppers (a wooden bottom with a scrap of tarpaulin on top suspended by the foot); these were called Holzpantinen (wooden clogs). The third type was a shoe made of a wooden bottom and a tarpaulin upper, covering most of the foot and reinforced with scraps of leather; these were called Holzschulen (wooden shoes). These were the assorted shoe types produced especially for the Nazi concentration camps.

When prisoners were exterminated at Auschwitz, not only their clothing, but also their shoes were issued to other inmates.

Probably, the most well known aspect of concentration camp prisoner identification relates to the insignia used to indicate each specific "category" of prisoners. Precise identification symbols were added to the striped clothing: Triangle stars, as well as letters and dots in specific colors symbolizing the category the prisoner belonged to (i.e. Nationality, Jews, Jehovah's Witnesses and clergy, political prisoners, common criminals, delinquents, homosexuals or any other particular group, such as escape-prone prisoners).

(48b) Adapted from "I Promise To Come Back" written and Illustrated by Shira Underberger. A student who had heard Anuta's story and made a children's book.

From Wikipedia. Forced labor under German rule during World War II, accessed 7/12/13.

(49) Panikos Panayi, "Exploitation, Criminality, Resistance. The Everyday Life of Foreign Workers and Prisoners of War in the German Town of Osnabrück, 1939-49," Journal of Contemporary History Vol. 40, No. 3 (Jul., 2005), pp. 483-502 in JSTOR.

From Wikipedia. Battle of Hamburg, accessed 7/12/13.

(50) "The Cabinet Papers 1915–1978: Glossary - B". The National Archives. Retrieved 2009-06-10.

(51) "The Forgotten Holocaust", by Richard C. Lukas, The University Press of Kentucky and "The Jews and the Poles in World War II" by Stefan Korbonski, Hippocrene Books.

(52) In Neugraben was a subcamp of the Nazi concentration camp Neuengamme. On September 13, 1944 the women's subcamp was opened in Falkenbergweg. 500 Czechish-Jewish women coming from the Ghetto Theresienstadt were deported to the Auschwitz concentration camp. The SS in Auschwitz selected the women for labor in Hamburg. In the Neugraben camp the work was building auxiliary homes, also laying supply pipes and building streets in the neighborhood Falkenbergsiedlung.

During the last months of World War II, some of the women had to do clearing up work in Hamburg's oil industry and to dig antitank obstacles in Hamburg-Hausbruch.

(53) In February 1945, the SS transferred the women to the camp Hamburg-Tiefstack and later from there to the Bergen-Belsen concentration camp.

(54) Klinkerwerk (brick factory) of the DEST

From: http://www.kz-gedenkstaette-neuengamme.de

(55) Tattoos and numbers: The System of identifying prisoners at Auschwitz. (http://www.ushmm.org)

(58) Mark Weber, historian and author, is director of the Institute for Historical Review. Encyclopaedia Judaica, Vol. 4, p. 610; Gedenkbuch: Opfer der Verfolgung der Juden unter der nationsozialistischen Gewaltherrschaft (Koblenz: Bundesarchiv, 1986; 2 vols.), pp. 1761-1762

(59) http://www.bergenbelsen.co.uk

(58) From Wikipedia. Forced labor under German rule during World War II, accessed 7/12/13

(60)   *U.S. Holocaust Memorial Museum; Encyclopedia Britannica; Simon Wiesenthal Center Multimedia Learning Center Online; Georgia Tech Library; United States Holocaust Memorial Museum; "Rebirth after the Holocaust: The Bergen-Belsen Displaced Persons Camp, 1945-1950."*

Marion A. Stahl